RESOURCE MOBILISATION THROUGH SHGs IN URBAN VILLAGES

About the Author

Dr. Chittaranjan Dash is educated at North Eastern Hill University, Shillong; Delhi University, Delhi; Utkal University, Bhubaneswar; Jawaharlal Nehru University, New Delhi and National Institute of Financial Management, Faridabad. He has contributed many research papers in national and international fora and academic journals. In year 2008, National Institute of Financial Management sponsored an international attachment at International Centre for the Promotion of Enterprises, Ljubljana (Slovenia) to study the business and financial developments in Europe. He has also authored a book entitled "*Social Ecology and Demographic Structure: Narratives and Discourses*" (2006). He joined Orissa Finance Service in 2004 and presently Deputy Director-cum-Faculty at Madhusudan Das Regional Academy of Financial Management, Government of Orissa, Bhubaneswar.

RESOURCE MOBILISATION THROUGH SHGs IN URBAN VILLAGES

Chittaranjan Dash

CONCEPT PUBLISHING COMPANY PVT. LTD.,
NEW DELHI-110059

ISBN-13 : 978-81-8069-828-6

First Published 2012

Published and Printed by

Concept Publishing Company Pvt. Ltd.
A/15-16, Commercial Block, Mohan Garden
New Delhi-110059 (India)
T: 25351460, 25351794, *F*: 091-11-25357109
E: publishing@conceptpub.com, W: www.conceptpub.com
Editorial Office: H-13, Bali Nagar, New Delhi-110 015, India.

Cataloging in Publication Data--*Courtesy:* D.K. Agencies (P) Ltd. <docinfo@dkagencies.com>

Dash, Chittaranjan.
Resource mobilisation through SHGs in urban villages / Chittaranjan Dash.
p. cm.
Includes bibliographical references (p.) and index.
ISBN 978-81-8069-828-6

1. Microfinance—India—Delhi. 2. Self-help groups—India—Delhi. 3. Resource allocation—India—Delhi. 4. Poor—Government policy—India—Delhi. 5. Community development—India—Delhi. 6. SHG-Bank Linkage Programme (India). I. Title. II. Title: Resource mobilisation through self-help groups in urban villages.

DDC 332.095456 23

Dedicated to

National Institute of Financial Management, Faridabad.

Foreword

World over microfinance has morphed into one of the most important instruments for fighting poverty. Though microfinance per se is not a silver bullet for battling poverty, its contribution to poverty reduction is almost universally recognized. In India microfinance has shown exponential growth in the last two decades. Though there are diverse models for purveying microfinance in the country and the financing institutions have the freedom to choose any model for microfinance delivery, the Self-Help Group (SHG)-Bank linkage programme has emerged as the predominant microfinance delivery model in the country. The SHGs have not only facilitated easy access to financial services for its members but also brought about a significant transformation in their socio-economic profile.

This study on 'Resource Mobilization through SHGs in Urban Villages' by Dr. Chittaranjan Dash attempts an in depth analysis of the role played by SHGs in collaboration with the NGOs and the banks in transforming lives of the poor in the urban villages. Based on a sample survey of selected urban villages in Delhi, the study sheds light on the needs and requirements of the urban poor and how their socio-economic life has been integrated and transformed by active participation in the SHG movement.

The author has highlighted the role played by the voluntary organizations in organising the poor through hand holding and strengthening their capacity to move out of poverty despite vulnerability, lack of assets and very low level of empowerment. The initiatives taken by the NGOs in areas of woman empowerment, women's literacy, gender sensitization, fight against atrocities on women and girl child have also been highlighted by the author. The author clearly articulates that women empowerment is the major contribution of microfinance movement. The study, however, underscores the need for much higher level of commitment and effective business models on part of banks and other apex level development institutions to reap the full potential of the SHG-Bank linkage programme in the urban areas. This assumes critical importance for inclusive growth given the fact that while urban population is increasing rapidly the outreach of microfinance in urban areas is very insignificant today. The book also brings out the need for integrated development activities to minimize the urban rural divide with reference to the major social indicators like poverty, education, employment and empowerment.

I hope this book would be a meaningful addition to the growing literature on microfinance and would prove useful to a wide section of readers including volunteers of the NGOs, bankers, researchers and policy makers.

Mumbai
July 11, 2011

H.R. Khan
Deputy Governor
Reserve Bank of India

Preface

Resources have been defined in many ways, depending on the ideological position of the scholars. The concern of the author of this book is in no way different from others. However, attempts have been made to liberate the concept 'resource' from the narrow anthropocentric views and make it an inclusive one. Here resource means every thing that makes of our environment, which are culturally acceptable, economically feasible, technologically accessible, environmentally sustainable and contribute in creating the material bases for the realization of meaningful existence. But, there is difference between availability of resources and their mobilization.

Resource mobilization, the central theme of the book, is a complex process. It depends upon factors ranging from the psychological make up of an individual to the social, cultural, political, economic and technological factors at a given point of time. Moreover, the specific characteristic features of a particular resource too play significant role in its mobilization.

Mobilization of financial resources has always been a major challenge in the history of modern world system. In the initial stages the financial resources were mobilized as seed capital through what is popularly known as primitive capital accumulation. Most of the time, profits generated through bilateral and multilateral trade, along with taxes, dues, duties, fines remittances, etc. mostly from the colonies, were the major sources of financial accumulation. Subsequently, it was the bank capital that helped in overcoming one of the major financial crises of industrial capitalism in the late 19th and early 20th century. Many scholars are of the opinion that the union of the bank and the industrial capital and the subsequent export of financial capital to the other countries in search of higher rates of return were the basis for the emergence of imperialism.

It was expected that after the independence of the colonies there would be some structural changes in the mobilization of the financial resource. But, the experiences of the post-colonial period, particularly in the country like India, showed that the Bretton Woods Institutions like the International Monetary Fund and the World Bank continued to have a major say in matters of financial resource mobilization world over. Every country had attempted to create their own institutional network for the same. Though these were apparently different and autonomous, yet in terms of their structural mechanism there were hardly any significant differences. All the institutions were busy in mobilizing financial resources on a large scale and most often than not these exercises were carried on by the state bureaucracy or financial experts. Consequently, the objects of true independence remained evasive to most of the people, largely because the terms and conditions imposed by these financial institutions were so stringent that most of the people went back to the traditional moneylenders and village *Shahookars*. Attempts were made to break the impasses created by the legal framework that mediated the interaction between the financial institutions and the people and in 1969 a major step was initiated through nationalization of banks in India. But, the situation did not change much. Seeing the apathy and lack of enthusiasm among the masses, the Reserve Bank of India opened National Bank for Agriculture and Rural Development (NABARD) in 1982 through the special Act of Parliament. The main objectives of this institution were to reach the poor agricultural populations living in the villages and minimize their miseries that they were facing from the exploitative financial and credit network created by the village moneylenders.

The outcome of this enterprise was far from satisfactory. In the meanwhile, the experience from Bangladesh, particularly its Grameen Bank, under the leadership of Muhammad Yunus, brought in new dimensions in the field of financial resource mobilization. The success of this enterprise lies in its ability to go for a paradigm shift from giant financial institutions like the Bretton Woods Institutions and Nationalized Banks to microfinance.

The present book written by Dr. Chittaranjan Dash is also an attempt in this direction but with many distinctive features of its own. The distinction of this work lies in extending the relevance of the micro-credit from its traditional rural settings to rural and urban areas within an urban centre.

The history of Delhi, the capital of India, is that of coming into prominence and disappearing into oblivion nearly eight times in the past. From the ancient capital at Indraprastha, and Anangpur founded by Anangpal to New Delhi, the capital of British India as well as the Indian Rebublic, this capital city had changed its location nearly to eight different places within the city under different rulers. Consequently, the present state of Delhi has urban as well as several villages within its administrative boundaries. The villages are governed by their own traditional laws and customs as well as the laws of the three urban local bodies, i.e., the Municipal Corporation of Delhi (MCD), the New Delhi Municipal Council (NDMC) and the Delhi Cantonment Board (DCB). There are villages that are situated at the periphery of the urban areas, but also there are village that are surrounded by the urban centers from all sides.

Financial resource mobilization in such a situation is a unique and challenging experience. In this book two sets of villages were selected from Najafgarh area of Delhi. The study of microfinance has been done by taking the case study of the institutions of Microfinance, i.e., the Self-Help Group (SHG).

The book is divided into seven chapters. First Chapter conceptualizes the institutions of microfinance in the social, historical and economic environment of the study area. It also brings out experiences of other scholars and planners related to the success of microfinance in other parts of the world. The contribution made by the Grameen Bank in Bangladesh, and particularly the visionary leadership of Muhammad Yunus has been probed with a critical viewpoint and utility of such experiences in case of urban villages in Delhi has received specific mention in the study. Chapter two shows the diagrammatic presentations of the morphology of the microfinance in the study, and the SHG-Bank linkage models of NABARD are the specific aspects of the study that has been correlated and contextualised after detailed field study. Moreover, this chapter also includes the survey of literature and the foresight it provided in conceptualizing the present study.

Chapter three deals with the problem of the paucity of data on such themes and tries to bridge the gap by generating the data through field survey. As mentioned previously, the villages in the study fall into two groups. There are villages that are at the periphery and there are other villages that are surrounded by urban areas. These villages are different in terms of their social composition and needs and requirement of the residents. Special care was taken to include variations in the social profile, educational qualifications, economic status and access to the microfinance of each respondent from these two sets of villages.

The performance of the microfinance in relation to socio-demographic parameters of the SHG members has been done in the fourth chapter. The economic profiles of the SHG members and spatial linkages of the sample villages find importance in the fifth chapter. The impact assessment of microfinance through credit and asset structure of the SHG members has been done in chapter six. The final chapter deals with the most vital aspects of microfinance and empowerment. It is vital because it is only through the microfinance that the issue of empowerment is properly addressed. The example from Bangladesh shows that the impact of microfinance has helped in improving female literacy and falling fertility. This was a major challenge before the Mullahs and they vehemently attacked the microfinance institutions and workers. In the present study there are no such outcomes that could be compared to the experience from Bangladesh. However, there is no doubt that the wind of change for better is in the offing. And if that happens, Dr. Dash's work, first of its own kind, will go in a long way in exploring the possibilities of a paradigm shift.

Microfinance is not about the size of the capital and number of the beneficiaries alone. In fact, it is much more than that. It is about the involvement of the people in their own terms and conditions to ameliorate their own conditions. It is about going for a paradigm shift from the giant financial institutions to small community level co-operations among the members. It is not about the marriage between the finance and industrial capital but between social and cultural capital with small economic assets.

Professor Balbir Singh Butola
Centre for the Study of Regional Development
School of Social Sciences
Jawaharlal Nehru University
New Delhi

Acknowledgements

This book came to fruition because of my sponsored study at the National Institute of Financial Management, Faridabad. In this book, I could use the data collected in connection with the study. In that sense, I am indebted to the institute.

I would like to acknowledge the Government of Orissa and the Planning Commission (Government of India) for sponsoring and funding the PGDBM (FM) programme at the National Institute of Financial Management, Faridabad, where I conducted the fieldwork among the Self-Help Group members to understand the role of microfinance in the urban context of Delhi.

I am grateful to Shri H.R. Khan, Executive Director, Reserve Bank of India for writing the foreword. I am also obliged to Shri Himanshu Ranjan Dash, Director, Madhusudan Das Regional Academy of Financial Management (MDRAFM), Bhubaneswar for his valuable suggestions while writing the book.

I feel indebted to my teachers Professor Balbir Singh Butola, Centre for the Study of Regional Development, School of Social Sciences, Jawaharlal Nehru University, New Delhi; Dr. Govind Singh Saun, Director, Indian Council for Social Science Research, New Delhi; Professor Sundar Singh Khanka, National Institute of Financial Management, Faridabad and Professor (Rtd.) Jyotirmayee Kanungo, Department of Anthropology, Utkal University, Bhubaneswar for their valuable guidance and cooperation in completion of this volume.

I am thankful to Mr. Shriom, Director, Model Rural Youth Development Organisation (MRYDO), Najafgarh, New Delhi and his staff, whom I interacted with and sought valuable suggestions at the time of carrying out field visits to the Self-Help Groups in and around Najafgarh area of Delhi.

I would like to thank my parents for their blessings, my wife Sangita and son Ishaan for their support and my brother-in-law Dr. Rajib Lochan Sahoo, AGM-*cum*-Archivist, College of Agricultural Banking, Reserve Bank of India, Punc and brother Dr. Manasranjan Dashmishra, Reader in Economics, Shri Vaishnav Institute of Management, Indore for their insights and guidance.

I would like to acknowledge the effort extended by Dr. Sugathan in correcting the Manuscript.

Special thanks are due for Mr. Ashok Kumar Mittal of Concept Publishing Company Pvt. Ltd., New Delhi for publishing the present volume.

Last but not the least, I express respect to the members of SHGs on whom I tested the academic queries. I am also thankful to the authors, researchers and World Wide Web whose works and ideas I used while doing my present humble academic and literary exercise.

Dr. Chittaranjan Dash

Contents

List of Tables

List of Figures

List of Photograph

List of Abbreviations

AAE	:	Average Annual Expenditure
AAI	:	Average Annual Income
AAR	:	Average Annual Return
ADB	:	Asian Development Bank
AIU	:	Association of Indian Universities
ARDC	:	Agricultural Refinance Development Corporation
ATMs	:	Automated Teller Machines
BPL	:	Below Poverty Line
CBI	:	Central Bank of India
DCW	:	Delhi Commission for Women
DDA	:	Delhi Development Authority
FIs	:	Financial Institutions
GOs	:	Government Officials
GRC	:	Gender Resource Centre
ICPE	:	International Centre for the Promotion of Enterprises
IETC	:	International Environmental Technology Centre
IRDP	:	Integrated Rural Development Programme
ISRDS	:	Integrated and Sustainable Rural Development Strategy
LIC	:	Life Insurance Corporation
MFIs	:	Microfinance Institutions
MRYDO	:	Model Rural Youth Development Organisation
MYRADA	:	Mysore Resettlement and Development Agency

NABARD	:	National Bank for Agriculture, Rural Development
NBFCs	:	Non-Banking Financial Institutions
NCR	:	National Capital Region
NCT	:	National Capital Territory
NGOs	:	Non-Governmental Organisations
NPPF	:	Non-Party Political Formation
PA	:	Private Agencies
PPP	:	Public Private Partnership
PRADAN	:	Professional Assistance for Development Action
RBI	:	Reserve Bank of India
RMK	:	Rashtriya Mahila Kosh
RRB	:	Regional Rural Bank
SAARC	:	South Asian Associations for Regional Cooperation
SBI	:	State Bank of India
SDP	:	State Domestic Product
SGSY	:	Swarnajayanti Gram Swarozgar Yojana
SHGs	:	Self-Help Groups
SHPIs	:	Self-Help Promotional Institutions
UCS	:	Urban Credit Society
UNEP	:	United Nations Environment Programme
UPAIs	:	Urban Poverty Alleviation Initiatives
VAs	:	Voluntary Associations
www	:	World Wide Web

1

Introduction

In the process of becoming and being "Homo sapiens sapiens" (the 'most' modern and civilized human beings), three major things happened: firstly, human beings tried to articulate their linguistic skills within and across different cultural boundaries which gave rise to various cognitive ideas; secondly, the domestication of anything and everything[1] made human beings prominent among other animals; and thirdly, resourcefulness. Resourcefulness, in this context, refers to managing the scarce resources. Finance[2] is one of the scarce resources[3] that human beings interact with. Finance is nothing but an art of managing money. Money is power because 'having or not having it' makes people different, i.e., weak or strong. Therefore, the strategy for the successful ones means to translate their limited resources into a better manner of use, which not only sustains them but also makes them look for a better future.

Every human society is associated with finance. Finance is the backbone of all activities. It has remained as an informal one not often making noticeable its intermingling aspect that how closely it has been netted with the life of people. Starting from birth, marriage and death, finance has been of prime importance. The ceremonial gift offered to the host party by the community is a kind of financial help extended to overcome with the burden of rites and rituals. For this matter, among the tribal communities, the villagers sacrifice their labour and manpower for the fellow ones, be it in house construction or harvesting paddy. In Islam, it is compulsory for the rich to sacrifice something for the poor. During the *haj* pilgrimage, relatives do help financially. Other religions do prescribe financing poor by the enabled ones. Therefore, the concept of microfinance is not new to the human society as it is based on the fundamental principle of proto-cooperation.[4] The precedence for microfinance lies in the numerous traditional and informal systems of credit that existed in human societies for centuries, long before modern commercial banking came to frontline. The present microfinance practices, in fact, have originated from the mutual credit transactions trust-based, peer-based, non-collateral borrowing and repayment.[5]

Human societies are heterogeneous in composition. Homogeneous society may be referred to a state where, one or two characteristics make a group at the micro level homogeneous. For example, a village may be homogeneous for caste, religion or race. However, class structure of a society is a complex phenomenon. The society is divisible into hierarchical order based on the economic capacity. Those who remain at the bottom of the hierarchy are known as marginalized, under-privileged and poverty stricken people. They are common to every human landscape, irrespective of the developing or developed nature of the world. Finance with reference to the bottommost category of the society may be termed as microfinance.

Pandey, a scholar on the subject states: "Microfinance as understood by its prefix 'micro' is essentially the provision of financial services to the poor who are otherwise deemed unfit by the conventional banking network. The prefix although explains the size of a unit of commodity or service delivered (i.e. finance extended per household/individual) to be small, however it does not further propagate compensating the same with large volumes of the commodity or service being catered to the burgeoning demand from the urban poor."[6]

According to the Asian Development Bank (ADB), "Microfinance is the provision of a broad range of financial services such as deposits, loans, payment services, money transfers and insurance to poor and low income households and their microenterprises."[7] Microfinance may also be defined, according to United Nations Environment Programme

(UNEP), as "programmes that extend small loans to very poor people for self-employment projects that generate income, allowing them to care for themselves and their families. Microfinance is the extension of small loans to entrepreneurs too poor to qualify for traditional bank loans."[8] Microfinance has proven an effective and popular measure in poverty alleviation programmes, enabling those without access to formal lending institutions to borrow at competitive rates and start small business, as UNEP has rightly argued. Schreiner and Colombet define microfinance as "the attempt to improve access to small deposits and small loans for poor households neglected by banks."[9]

Definitions of microfinance differ from country to country. Some of the criteria of microfinance generally used include first, with reference to size, the loans are micro or very small in size; second, the target users are micro-entrepreneurs and low-income households; third, the funds are utilised for income generation, enterprise development and also for community use towards health, education etc.; and fourth, most of the terms and conditions for microfinance loans are flexible and easy to understand and are suited to the local conditions of the community.[10]

Microfinance has been canvassed since 1980s by different agencies of the world for the reason being it covers the uncovered elements of the society; the attention was left to a great extent by the macro-financial policies. The success of microfinance brings the state to reassess its developmental credit initiatives of the past. There is a sign of withdrawal by the state from the subsidy based credit approach, and it encourages the participatory-based credit. Formal banks do not support much of the credit requirement of the poor, the reason being that they cannot offer collaterals to the banks for the credit. "Banks were given heavy subsidies, not only to keep interest rates low, but to compensate for the high transaction costs and inherent risks of such operations."[11] All these could not help keep the repayment rates high and default rates low. "The enviable success of microfinance programmes in terms of high repayment rates has mostly been attributed to the group lending aspect with the much-celebrated 'joint liability' feature."[12] Countries, like India, now face a transition from state-centred development to community-centred and now to individual-centred development.

One of the studies depicts that the Integrated and Sustainable Rural Development Strategy (ISRDS) is designed to realize a vision that will provide "rural communities with viable institutions, sustainable economies and universal access to social amenities" and them able to "attract and retain skilled and knowledgeable people, ... equipped to contribute to growth and development."[13] Sustainable development[14] aims to "use resource in a way so that, human needs could be fulfilled in present as well as future. The prime elements of sustainable development are economy, society and environment."[15] Steps are being taken by governments to ensure sustainable development across the entire spectrum.

Governments all over the world have focused upon sustainable rural development[16] in an organized way. Rural locations in particular, need more economic development in order to match urban centric development. All the spheres of development including economic, social, cultural have primarily benefitted urban locations. Even in case of industrial growth, urban places got best of growth and prosperity. Many actions have been taken to fill this chasm between rural and urban growth. Poverty in rural areas has remained by and large, the main focal point of governments and development agencies. Sustainable rural development is the most effective way to eliminate this curse. To improve the standard of living, governments have allocated more financial muscle for the rural areas. To maintain sustainable rural development, several regional development agencies, national governments, international development organizations and NGOs are putting in their best efforts.[17]

For years the financial institutions have catered to the needs of people who could provide collaterals to the institutions. The financial institutions have tried to reduce the risk of default. The scrutiny and authentication of customers has been the priority for them. However, with all the necessary steps taken, the institutions could not reduce the mounting bad debt. Rather, this pressure has been increasing day by day. Then, the question arises here is that who is a better customer for the financial institution, whether the *bona fide* customer who sleeps over the debt carelessly or who has not been looked at by the institutions but could do better if the chance has been extended to the needy one. Our society, by and large, is of heterogeneous composition. A substantial proportion of people of our society do not have resources for approaching the financial institutions. This is the reality for India and other developing countries. Thus, time has come to bring forth the uncovered customers to the forefront of the financial institutions.

People-centred principles have influenced the course of western culture, often changing the bearings of education, business, public policy and international relief and development programmes. In international relief and development organizations, however, people-centred practice became 'participatory development'. Participation has been variously described as a means and an end, as essential within agencies as it is in the field and as an educational and empowering process necessary to correct power imbalances between rich and poor. It has been broadly conceived to embrace the idea that all 'stakeholders' should take part in decision-making and it has been described to make use of local knowledge to design programmes.[18]

Microfinance is essentially the small financial benefits extended to the poor. In the year 1979, the Indian Council of Medical Research stipulated that the poor people are those people who do not meet to consume 2100 and 2400 calories in their diet daily in the urban and rural areas respectively. Although the branch network of the formal financial institutions expanded rapidly beginning the early 1970s, a large segment of such poor population remains outside the banking fold, especially for its credit requirements. This led to the search for alternative policies and mechanisms for reaching out to the poor to satisfy their felt needs. In this context, microfinance interventions were recognised all over the world as an effective tool that could raise incomes, contribute to individual and household security and change social relations for the better.[19]

Microfinance has grown rapidly since the late 1990s for the following reasons: *first,* ability to reach out to the poor; *second,* promise of financial sustainability; *third,* the potential to build on traditional systems; *fourth,* provision of informal and flexible financial services to the poor for meeting their modest consumption and livelihood needs; *fifth,* the availability of better financial products as a result of experimentation and innovation; and *sixth,* provision for collateral-free micro-credit to the poor. Microfinance is helpful for the poor, who meet their need for small credit and other financial services. These services offered to low-income borrowers for meeting their needs have made the microfinance movement grow at rapid pace in India.[20]

In Bangladesh, the Grameen Bank was established in the year 1983 as a formal bank by the leadership of Professor Muhammad Yunus. "Gradually a new word, 'microcredit', was coined for these kinds of collateral-free loans for income-generating activities of the poor. The *Grameen*[21] idea spread all over the world."[22] Today, there are more than 59 countries, both in developing and developed world, where *Grameen* type credit programmes are being replicated.[23] With reference to Bangladesh, some scholars argue that "Grameen Bank's micro-lending is sustainable because its borrowers are viable: loans have a positive effect on wages, dropout rates are low at about 5 per cent and repayment is above 90 per cent."[24]

Microfinance through institutional arrangement is a recent innovation for poverty reduction among the poor. Resource mobilisation through small loans or microcredit as such is not new. It has been prevailing in several countries by way of individual arrangements through moneylenders. The concept of money lending has been institutionalised, rationalised and reformed for sustainability of both the borrowers and the lenders. The genesis of cooperative society or a credit union type of social arrangement of the poor for thrift deposits and borrowing was initial intermediation of non-collateral credit services to the poor. But its performance and outreach was not satisfactory due to its style of management.[25]

Basically in a developing country like India, where 70 per cent of its citizen stay in rural areas, attention of the government used to be rural centric in order to take care of alleviating poverty and other socio-economic problems. Many programmes and policies were drawn to curb this menace. However, a few were successful. The unsuccessful ones rather weakened the financial institutions destined for the poor and rural areas. The share of the formal financial sector in total rural credit was little above 50 per cent compared to informal finance at almost 40 per cent in the early 1990s. "At this juncture it was apparent that there was an urgent need for financial innovation in the rural credit markets in India. It was also in such environment that microfinance emerged as an innovation the world over."[26]

First official interest in informal group lending in India took shape during 1986-87 on the initiative of the National Bank for Agriculture and Rural Development (NABARD). As a part of this broad mandate, NABARD initiated certain research projects on Self-Help Groups (SHGs) as a channel for delivery of microfinance in the late 1980s.[27] The policy interest in the whole concept of SHG linkage with banks was institutionalised with the Reserve Bank of India (RBI) establishing in 1994 a working group on NGOs and SHGs comprising representatives from NABARD, Bankers and development practitioners.[28]

There are two ways of looking at the Indian society; one is rural and the other one is urban. They are like two pans of the balance. Any step-motherly attitude would disturb the balancing act of the society. The underdeveloped rural areas remain one of the prime aspects of concern. The rural areas are not able to accommodate the demand of the labour folk. As a result, the push-pull factor[29] is the reason for which the imbalance is created. The unstoppable migration of people from rural to urban areas creates havoc leading to mushrooming of slums, congestions, diseases, crimes, etc. The central issue becomes urban poverty. Therefore, withdrawing attention from this aspect of development and ignoring the urban poor from their development would seriously harm the social opportunities, and thus creating an imbalance therein.

Therefore, the space is now created for these stateless urban people to think of microfinance, which can bring a bit of relief in the management of their life and family.

The urban poor are heterogeneous in composition. The place of origin, caste, religion, language and the overall background of socialisation are some of the elements that make the urban poor too much heterogeneous. The occupations that they carry out in urban locations also differ from what they ought to do at the place of their origin. The social connection as such becomes a vacuum for them. The day and night become a passing time for them, as the target is to fill up their empty vessel. Absolutely for them, there is no room to think of savings and credit. Even if they think of any credit, is there any financial institution ready to provide them any credit? At this position introducing microfinance for the stateless urban poor probably help at surpassing the critical juncture of life.

Urban Microfinance

Urban centres and cities do display unique personality of the land. Their personality is an outcome of the environment, socio-cultural and economic set up of the land to which they are surrounded by. These factors decide the activities of the people and their occupation. Thus, for example, the coastal urban centres and hill stations, religious cities and modern cities, commercial cities and mining cities, port cities and urban areas in hinterland, etc. display different requirements. The requirements of urban microfinance do change depending on the characteristics of urban centres. For that matter, the economic activities of Self-Help Groups (SHGs) in religious cities would differ from the port cities. What I intend to advocate here is that there is a basic urban character which is common to all urban centres along with their unique urban personality, which is an outcome of historical and ethnographic traditions.

It is estimated that the country will have more than 40 per cent of its population in urban centres by the year 2030. While the number of rural poor decreased from 25.7 crores (257 million) to 19.3 crores (193 million) between 1991 and 2001, the number of urban poor actually increased from 5.2 crores (52 million) to 6.7 crores (67 million). Despite the large number of urban poor, most of them have little or no access to formal financial services. There is relatively little outreach of microfinance in major urban areas.[30]

Urban areas are bound to be the centre of economic activities with a variety of microenterprises. These microenterprises are more often relying on informal financial sources for their business and consumption loan. Informal sources do charge exorbitant interest ranging between 60 per cent and 300 per cent per annum. There is ample opportunity to provide loans through microfinance institutions comparatively at a lesser rate. They can enhance their profit through lower cost of capital and can build assets over a period of time by additional income. Socio-economic backgrounds of urban poor people are different in various aspects than their rural counterparts. Apart from the problem of rapid urbanization, there is a huge need to generate livelihood opportunities for migrant population from rural areas.[31]

Urban Microfinance has not been as pervasive as its rural counterpart to capture the urban poor market comprising of 35 to 40 per cent of population as per 2001 Census of India with only a dismal 0.01 per cent having banking relationships. The business strategy of volume-induced growth is however only a later realization proceeded by more fundamental roadblocks captured by the socio-economic composition of the urban poor.[32]

There are three basic problems regarding the study of Urban Microfinance. *Firstly,* there are no clear estimates of the number of people in urban areas with any access to organised financial services. This may be attributed, in part at least, to the migratory nature of the urban poor, comprising mostly of migrants from rural areas. Even moneylenders often shy away from lending to urban poor. *Secondly,* there have been a few instances of Microfinance Institutions (MFIs) venturing into this area of lending to urban poor, who are undertaking micro-enterprises and small business activities. Urban branches of banks, even though having manpower and technology support, are not attuned to SHG lending or microfinance. *Thirdly,* at present, NABARD is permitted, as per its Act and Mandate, to support microfinance activities in rural and semi-urban areas only. An enabling provision has to be made in the NABARD Act, 1981 permitting the NABARD to provide microfinance services to the urban poor.[33]

As per Census of India 2001, the urban poor comprise around 35 to 40 per cent of the population, but only 0.01 per cent of them have banking relationships.[34] While rural areas account for up to 95 per cent of current microfinance outreach in India, its cities are completely un-served.[35] In spite of large network of bank branches and Automated Teller Machines (ATMs) that exist in cities, many of the poor find their financial needs largely unmet due to lack of documentation, regular incomes, and a low degree of comfort in visiting banks for transactions. As a result, urban poor feel forced to rely on informal credit from moneylenders who demand interest as high as 10 per cent per day from borrowers. In urban areas, lack of access to basic services and productive inputs, trading space for vendors, and skill and livelihood training further pushes the poor into poverty, in spite of their status as an essential component of the country's workforce.[36] Informal credit helps the poor to manage cash flow, particularly unexpected expenditure. Supply of this credit ranges from the infamous moneylenders, pawnbrokers and relatives. The informal market offers the urban poor access and convenience. However, they pay a high price to borrow from many of these sources and end up being indebted for long period of time.[37] It is also evident that the dynamics and challenges in the urban environment vis-à-vis microfinance are unique and distinct from rural areas. Thus, providing urban microfinancial services can be a tremendous opportunity, given the gravity of the prevailing situation, existing demand and expanding market. In the 2001 Census, Delhi occupies the first place with 93.01 per cent of people living in urban areas.

The urbanisation process of Delhi has a chequered history. If one goes by the historical evidences, Delhi has reason to prominence and losing into oblivion more than a dozen times in its known historical past. It is interesting to know that in all these phases, the core of Delhi has shifted from one place to another. In the ancient past, the core of Delhi was *Indraprastha*. It was *Anangpur* during Anangpal,[38] a *Rajput* of *Anangpur* village who founded the city of Delhi. *Lalkot* was the first city of Delhi (1052 AD) during the *Tomar Rajput* king by the name of Raja Delu.[39]

Muhammad of *Ghor* conquered Delhi in twelfth century AD. He was followed by the *Turkish* and the *Pathan* dynasties: the *Slaves*, the *Khiljis*, the *Tughlaks*, the *Sayyids* and the *Lodis*. Subsequent to all came the *Mughals*.[40] During the time of *Slaves* (1192-1287 AD), the cores were *Hauz Shami, Mehrauli and Kilokri*. When the *Khiljis* (1290-1316 AD) had ruled, these were *Siri* and *Hauz Khas*. At the time of *Togloqu* dynasty (1320-1398 AD), the cores were *Togloquabad*, *Adilabad* and *Ferozabad*. During *Lodis* (1451-1526 AD), these were *Lodi* estate, *Zamrudpur* and *Muhammadpur*. During the *Mughal* Empire (1526-1803 AD), the cores were shifted to *Salimgarh*, *Jahangirpuri* and *Shahjahanabad*.[41] In colonial times, it was *Raisina Hills*. As a result of that the epicentre of administration of Delhi does not have a fixed region. In other words, a capital region was comprised of many centres. Ultimately in 1911, Delhi was chosen as the capital of British India, and subsequently the capital of independent India in the year 1947. It ensembles all the ancient city centres and the villages surrounding it.

According to the 1961 census survey, there were as many as 300 villages in Delhi. After independence, when Delhi became the national capital, there was rapid increase in activities. It started expanding in demographic, geographic, economic and administrative functions. All the villages in the periphery are incorporated to Delhi. Over these years, a large influx of people moving from depressed and distressed rural India moved to urban centres for better opportunities and used Delhi as a shelter zone in the form of slums, the old villages and peripheral villages. These locations, i.e., the peripheral villages, old villages and slums got only marginal benefits of urban amenities and created a demand for urban amenities and facilities. It is here the whole issue of urban microfinance gets enhanced significance.

To sum up, microfinance may be defined as programmes that extend small loans to very poor people for self-employment projects that generate income, allowing them to care for themselves and their families. Microfinance is the extension of small loans to entrepreneurs too poor to qualify for traditional bank loans. Microfinance is the provision of a broad range of financial services such as deposits, loans, payment services, money transfers, and insurance to poor and low-income households and their micro-enterprises. Urban microfinance has not been as pervasive as its rural counterpart to capture the urban poor market comprising of 35-40 per cent of population as per 2001 census of India with only a dismal 0.01 per cent having banking relationships. The growth of microfinance in India has also to be seen in the light of financial sector reforms in India starting from 1991 and the global emphasis on commercialisation of the sector. There is a surge in interest currently among both the MFIs and banks to extend micro lending to urban areas. The NABARD is yet to amend its Act to go in this direction. Though there are different models for purveying micro-finance, the SHG-Bank Linkage Programme has emerged as the major microfinance programme in the country. Urban Microfinance certainly needs a different approach than rural operations. The process and methodology should be built on the basis of client's needs and preferences. Socio-economic backgrounds of urban poor people are different in various aspects than their rural counterparts. There are a few constraints for which urban microfinance has yet to take the pace; firstly, there are no clear estimates of the number of people in urban areas with any access to organised financial services. Secondly, there have been a few instances of MFIs venturing into this area of lending to urban poor who are undertaking micro-enterprises and small business activities. Thirdly, at present, the NABARD is permitted, as per its Act and Mandate, to support microfinance activities in rural and semi-urban areas only. Therefore, the present book aims at studying the microfinance in the context of Enclave and Peripheral Villages of Delhi.

NOTES AND REFERENCES

1. Everything here refers not only to animals and agriculture, but also germination of ideas and wisdoms, which brought science and technology to work in favour of human beings. Man is the only animal who can modify the environment by managing the resources available to him.
2. "Finance is the science and practice of raising and expending revenues" (Shashi, 1992:202).
3. In modern times, management of financial resources is a crucial issue. There are two ways by which resources are to be managed such as, when there is enough finance, or with scarce resources or limited finance. The gamut of economics surrounds the management of scarce resources. In other words, it is the management of limited resources for satisfying the unlimited wants. Earning money is not so important; it is the spending of money. Even for the poor, the resources are too limited. They do not compete for the comfort or luxury; they mad-rush for the survival. It is difficult for them to swim against the current created by the giants of the market. They are operating as if in an alien territory abiding the rules of the game. Therefore, microfinance is important in the present context.
4. Fundamentally, human society, irrespective of its stages of development, behaves as a proto-cooperative society. There is an intricate network of relationship among the human members based on mutual trust and sympathy. The degree of proto-cooperation varies with the stages of development.
5. United Nations Environment Programme (UNEP) (2003): *'Microfinance in the Urban Environmental Development Perspective'*, International Environmental Technology Centre. p. 4, found at *www.unep.or.jp/ietc/focus/Microfinance-interlinkages.doc.*
6. V. Pandey (2007): 'Urban Microfinance—Efforts towards a Lasting Impact', *Microfinance Focus,* Vol. 2, No. 1, p. 4, found at http://www.karmayog.org/redirect/strred.asp?docId=10337.
7. Asian Development Bank (ADB) (2000): *Finance to the Poor: Microfinance Development Strategy*. Manila: ADB. p. 2.
8. UNEP (2003): p. 3.
9. M. Schreiner and H.H. Colombet (2001): 'From Urban to Rural: Lessons for Microfinance from Argentina', *Development Policy Review,* Vol. 19, No. 3, p. 339.
10. UNEP (2003): p. 3.
11. S. Bera (2008): 'Programme Design and Impact Assessments: 'Success' of Microfinance in Perspective', *Economic and Political Weekly,* Vol. 43, No. 32, p. 77.
12. *Ibid.* p. 77.

13. 'The Integrated Sustainable Rural Development Strategy (ISRDS)' (2000) found at http://www.info.gov.za/otherdocs/2000/isrds.pdf.
14. Generally, 'Sustainable Development' is defined in terms of judicious use of resource to satisfy the needs of present generation without compromising the quality of life of future generation (Brundtland Commission Report, 1987: 43-46). Sustainable development in case of financial resources could be conceptualised in such a way that the mobilization of financial resources from the internal and external sources is to meet the needs of the present generation without mortgaging the opportunities of the future generation.
15. 'Index of Sustainable Development' found at http://www.mumbaispace.com/sustainabledevelopment.
16. 'Sustainable rural development' generally, means that the resource base of rural areas is not to be allowed to deteriorate for the development of urban areas. "Many past development policies have been based on the idea of a rush for growth. Sustainable development stresses the importance of permanent growth and development" (Pearce and Warford, 1993:29-30).
17. 'Index of Sustainable Development' found at http://www.mumbaispace.com/sustainabledevelopment.
18. R. Jennings (2000): 'Participatory Development as New Paradigm: The Transition of Development Professionalism' October, Prepared for the "Community Based Reintegration and Rehabilitation in Post-Conflict Settings" Conference Washington, DC found at http://www.usaid.gov/our_work/cross-cutting_programs/transition_initiatives/pubs/ptdv1000.pdf.
19. Reserve Bank of India (2008): *Annual Report 2007-08*. Mumbai: RBI, p. 192.
20. *Ibid*. pp. 192-93.
21. In replicating *Grameen,* one must remember right from the beginning that, if the recovery rate is not near 100 per cent, no matter how good it looks, it is not *Grameen*. It is essential to have a thorough understanding of how *Grameen* works, its philosophy and procedures (Yunus, 2007: 181). The *Grameen* principles (Yunus, 2004: 4077-78) are (i) *Grameen* believes that poverty is not created by the poor, but by the institutions and policies, which surround them; (ii) Charity is not the answer to poverty. It serves only to perpetuate poverty and create dependency; (iii) The *Grameen* system is built on the belief that there is no difference in the ability of a poor person and any other person. The poor merely do not get the opportunity to explore their potential and so their abilities remain unutilised or under-utilised. If they had the opportunity, they would be able to change their own lives; (iv) The *Grameen* principle has always been the less the person has, the higher the priority she gets. Whereas, the

conventional banks start with the principle that the more you have the more you get; (v) Lending to women brings greater benefits to the family than men. If the mother is the borrower, the children are the immediate beneficiaries.

22. M. Yunus (2004): 'Grameen Bank, Microcredit and Millennium Development Goals'. *Economic and Political Weekly,* Vol. 39, No. 36, p. 4077.
23. M. Yunus (2007): *Banker to the Poor.* New Delhi: Penguin Books. p. 182.
24. World Bank (1999): *Bangladesh: From Counting the Poor to Making the Poor Count,* Washington, D.C.: The World Bank, p. 44.
25. Md. S.H. Choudhury (2000): 'On Sustainable Microfinance Operations', In: *Microfinance: Emerging Challenges* (eds.) K. Basu and K. Jindal. New Delhi: Tata McGraw-Hill Publishing Company Ltd. p. 71.
26. P. Satish (2005): 'Mainstreaming of Indian Microfinance'. *Economic and Political Weekly,* Vol. XL, No. 17, p. 1731.
27. *Ibid.* p. 1732.
28. *Ibid.* p. 1733.
29. "Rural to urban migrants should not be considered merely as pawns pushed and pulled by macroeconomic forces but also as actors in a position to shape the urbanization process, so pavement dwellers in big cities should not be considered merely as the victims of dire poverty, but also as dynamic agents capable of implementing their own economic strategies and of finding appropriate responses to specific urban environments" (Dupont, 2000:99).
30. V. Kumar (2007): 'From Our Desk', *Microfinance Focus,* Vol. 2, No. 1, p. 3 found at http://www.karmayog.org/redirect/strred.asp?docId=10337.
31. *Ibid.* p. 3.
32. V. Pandey (2007): p. 4.
33. National Bank for Agriculture and Rural Development (NABARD) (2008): *Report on the Committee of Financial Inclusion.* Mumbai: NABARD. p. 17 found at *www.nabard.org/pdf/report_financial/Full%20Report.pdf.*
34. 'Reaching the Other 100 Million Poor in India', Centre for Micro Finance, India. 2006, found at *http://www.microfinancegateway.org/files/38966_file_20.pdf.*
35. S. Benerjee and S. Kumar (2007): Poverty Microfinance Community: Solution Exchange for the Microfinance Community Consolidating Reply, found at *http://www.msdf.org/priorities/MSDFIndiaMicrofinanceFinal.pdf.*
36. 'Reaching the Other 100 Million Poor in India', Centre for Micro Finance, India. 2006, found at *http://www.microfinancegateway.org/files/38966_file_20.pdf.*

37. Supriti, S.M. Barnhardt and R. Ramanathan (2002): '*Urban Poverty Alleviation in India: A General Assessment and a Particular Perspective*', Vol.1, Bangalore: Ramanathan Foundation, found at http://unpan1.un.org/intradoc/groups/public/documents/APCITY/UNPAN029047.pdf
38. Historians seem to differ on the point of the founder of the city of Delhi. According to Percival Spear, it was Anangpal of village *Anangpur*, a member of *Rajput* clan who founded the city of Delhi. The factor of security seems to be the main reason for the selection of such a barren and rocky terrain for the founding of a city. The village *Anangpur*, which is situated 30 kilometres south of Delhi and five kilometres south west of *Suraj Kund*, is on the quartzite tableland of *Aravali* (Verma, 2001:7-8).
39. U. Verma (2001): *Delhi: A Tale of Seven Cities*. New Delhi: Smriti Books, pp. 7-9.
40. *Ibid*. p. 98.
41. L. Peck (2005): *Delhi: A Thousand Years of Building*. New Delhi: The Lotus Collection, pp. ix-xii.

2

Contexualising Microfinance in General and Urban Microfinance in Particular

In this chapter an attempt has been made to understand the microfinance in the context of urban areas. Several issues regarding the microfinance are discussed in this chapter. Approaches to microfinance and microfinance models vis-à-vis NABARD's activities towards SHGs have also been discussed. In addition to this, the composition and *modus operandi* of SHGs along with advantages and issues regarding the groups have been highlighted in the context of rural and urban areas. Furthermore, the chapter also includes a survey of literature to enlighten the work of different scholars in this field.

Morphology of Microfinance

There are different approaches[1] through which the microfinance can be understood better. They are the Grameen and Solidarity Approach,[2] the Group Approach,[3] the Approach of Individual Credit,[4] the Community Banking Approach,[5] and the Approach of Credit Unions and Cooperatives.[6] Among these, "the group approach is familiar in India. Savings, loans, and loan repayments are taken care of at the group level"[7] (see Fig. 2.1). The group, basically, is known as Self-Help Group (SHG).[8] "SHGs are considered as one of the most significant tools to adopt participatory approach for the economic empowerment of women. It is an important institution for improving the life of women on various social components. The basic objective of an SHG is that it acts as the forum for members to provide space and support to each other."[9] "Self-Help Groups are defined as small groups, which are formed voluntarily with members who want to solve their common problems through mutual aid. Micro-credit means quantum of amount given for self-employment activities to members belonging to lower income groups. Whereas, the SHG is an institutional means to provide access to credit to poor people."[10]

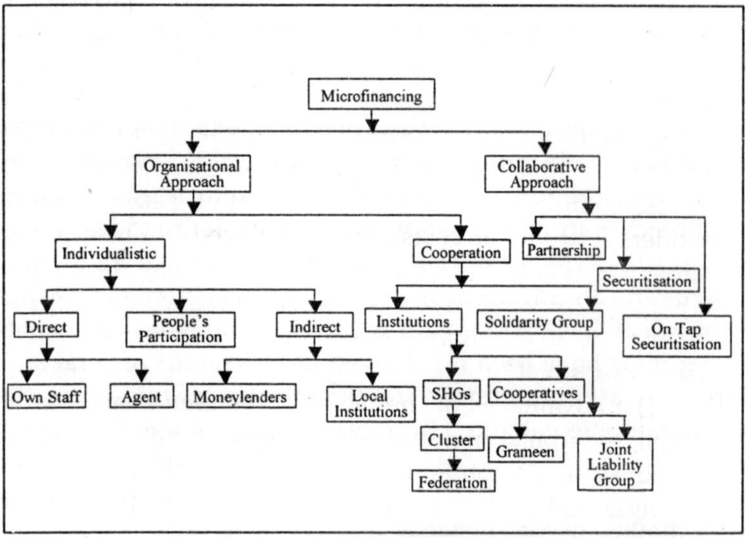

Fig. 2.1: Morphology of Microfinance

Source: Dasgupta (2005:1236).

The SHGs became a regular component of Indian financial system since 1996.[11] The SHGs are small, informal and homogeneous groups of not more than 20 members.[12] The homogeneous nature of the group ensures that the members do not have conflicting interests and can participate freely.[13] "The members have poor risk-taking ability, no collateral to offer and have limited earning opportunities. After its formation, the group regularly collects a fixed amount of thrift from each member. With this amount, it starts lending to members for petty consumption needs. Scarce resources and more demand for credit compel the group to make appropriate decisions. The working fund grows over time and after establishing its credibility,[14] the group can also approach Financial Institutions (FIs) for credit. The group keeps taking decisions as in the past but with more resources. As the whole, group is liable for the amount borrowed from the bank, its responsibility in monitoring the members increases."[15]

In the programmes related to group lending, "the functions of screening, monitoring and enforcement of repayment, to a large extent, are transferred from the bank's agent to the borrowers, that is, the group members themselves. As compared to the socially and physically distant bank agents, group members can perform all such functions more effectively and at a relatively lower cost. The group members are able to access complex and sensitive information just like informal lenders. Transaction costs are thus reduced."[16] The group uses the money according to its requirement among the members. Therefore, the mismatch between demand and supply is minimised. In addition to this, there is also some flexibility of loan repayment.[17]

The advantages of the SHG can be seen from economic, social, environmental and technological point of view. SHG works as an economic unit. It is like a bank with an aim to savings, credits and returns for the members. As mentioned before the SHG is a homogeneous social unit. It is not only a platform to interact among members but also a place of sharing happiness, and sorrow, misery, misfortune, etc., a way to get rid of the latter. The members do exchange ideas about the indigenous knowledge basically relating to the craft mechanism. Therefore, the group is a unit reservoir of socio-cultural capital.[18] The group sometimes contributes time and strength for the welfare of neighbours and community. They often resolve conflicts and mistrust of theirs and others.

However, there are some basic issues regarding the operational aspect of microfinance. The success of microfinance depends on the attitude, commitment and sincerity of the group members. SHG is an informal group. The group is not backed by any legal sanction and agreement. No instrument lies with the group to resolve situations like any breach of trust, default, conflict and separation. In case of death of a member or a member runs away, there is no or little chance of recovery. This is a larger risk that the group has to carry always. There is no link with the behaviour of the market. Even if it is linked with the market, there is no speculation path. Investment is generally restricted to the group members only. Investment in terms of hedging is conspicuous by its absence. The knowledge for the investment process is either not found or nonexistent among the members. The share of microfinance is so negligible that it cannot form any impact on the movement of the market.

SHG-Bank Linkage Models of NABARD

"The SHG-Bank Linkage Programme can be regarded as the most potent initiative since independence for delivering financial services to the poor in a sustainable manner. The search for such alternatives started with internal introspection regarding the innovations which the poor had been traditionally making to meet their financial services needs. It was observed that the poor tended to come together in a variety of informal ways for pooling their savings and dispensing small and unsecured loans at varying costs to group members on the basis of need."[19]

NABARD was set up in July 1982 by the Act of Parliament to take over the functions of Agricultural Refinance Development Corporation (ARDC) and the refinancing functions of RBI in relation to cooperative banks and Regional Rural Banks (RRBs). Thus, NABARD plays a dual role as an apex institution and as a refinance institution.[20] In the year 1987, there was an attempt by the NABARD to search for alternative mechanism to improve the accessibility of the poor for financial services in a cost effective and sustainable manner. As a result, a delivery mechanism was developed to encompass financial relationship between informal organisations of the poor like the SHGs and formal organisations like banks. Subsequently, with the needed backup policy support from the Reserve Bank of India and the Central Government, the SHG-Bank Linkage Programme was launched by NABARD as a pilot project in February 1992.[21] There are certain objectives of the linkage programme such as (a) to evolve supplementary strategy for meeting the credit needs of the poor by combining informal sector credit system with formal credit institutions, (b) to build up mutual trust and confidence between the banker and the rural poor, (c) to encourage banking activity and (d) to improve flow of credit to rural poor with reduced transaction cost, both for the financing bank and the borrower.[22]

The pilot project was designed as a partnership model between three agencies, viz., the SHG, Banks and NGOs.[23] NGOs have played a commendable role in promoting SHGs and linking them with banks. NGOs, being local initiators with their low resources, are finding it difficult to expand in other areas and regions. There is, therefore, a need to evolve an initiative package, which should motivate these NGOs to diversify into other backward areas.[24] The SHG—Bank Linkage Programme has been growing rapidly and the number of SHGs financed increased to 29.25 lakhs (cumulative) on 31 March 2007.[25]

The SHG-Bank Linkage Programme shows uneven progress in different regions. Its better result has been linked to various factors like pro-active role of State Governments, presence of well performing NGOs, socio-cultural factors, better performance of SHGs, etc. Around 50 per cent of the linked SHGs are from southern region consisting of Andhra Pradesh, Karnataka, Kerala, and Tamil Nadu. Many states such as Uttar Pradesh and Bihar have shown poor performance under the programme. Similarly, there is a slow progress of the SHG-Bank Linkage movement in the North-eastern and Central parts of the country. It is even argued that the SHG strategy was not suitable to the social configurations that prevailed in the Northeast.[26]

There are certain issues on extending the SHG-Bank Linkage Scheme to urban areas. The issues are such as (i) there are no clear estimates of the number of poor people[27] in urban areas and their no accessibility to organised financial services;

(ii) urban branches of banks, even though having manpower and technology support, are not attuned to SHG lending or microfinance; and (iii) the multiple and diversified activities of the banks act as barrier to cater to the microfinance market segment.[28] In 2008, the Committee on Financial Inclusion[29] has recommended amendment to NABARD Act to enable it to provide microfinance services to the urban poor.

For SHG credit, there are three different models. As shown on the Figure No. 2.2, these are Model I: NABARD-Bank-SHG-Member (without NGO intervention), Model II: NABARD-Bank-SHG-Member (with NGO or SHG Promoting Institution, SHPI as facilitator) and Model III: NABARD-Bank-NGO (as financial intermediary or MFI)-SHG-Member.[30] In Model I, SHGs are formed and extended credit by the banks. In other words, bank itself acts as a SHPI. RRBs are getting involved largely in formulating this type of Model. In Model II, SHGs are formed by the NGOs but the banks extend credit. In other words, the facilitating agencies like NGOs, government agencies or other community-based organisations do act as SHPIs. In Model III, in addition to forming SHGs, NGOs avail bulk loan from banks for lending to SHGs. In other words, the SHPIs act as financial intermediaries between groups and banks. They promote the groups, nurture and train them and then approach banks for bulk loans for on-lending to SHGs. At aggregate level, Models I, II and III account for 20, 72 and 8 per cent of SHGs and 14, 81 and 5 per cent credit respectively.[31] Hence, Model II has been very popular in linking formal institutions with the SHGs through the help of SHPIs.

Review of Literature

Survey of literature is an important aspect of any research. The literature contributes information, fact and ideas. A thorough understanding of the literature enhances the research process. The sequential improvisation of events adds a better sketch in building arguments and streamlines the path to progress in the field. The survey enlightens the process of eventisation. The review is also a process to familiarise the scholars along

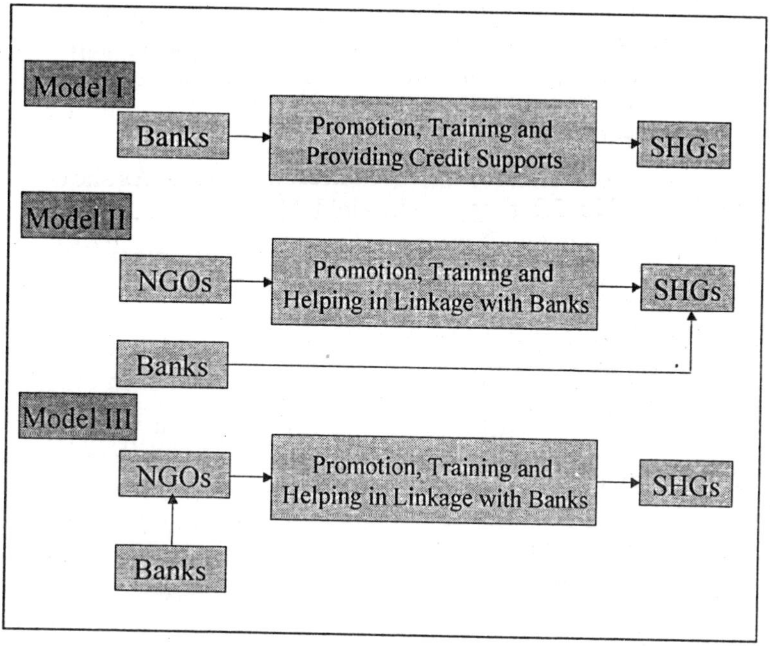

Fig. 2.2: SHG-Bank Linkage Models of NABARD

Source: Sarangi (2007:88).

with their scholarly contributions. Similarly, in understanding the process of microfinance with reference to urban areas, the review of literature has a greater role not only to build up arguments but also to venture further.

Microfinance means providing very poor families with very small loans (microcredit) to help them engage in productive activities or grows their tiny business. Overtime, microfinance has come to include a broader range of services credit, savings, insurance, etc. Since 1950s, experiments started but microcredit became prominent in 1980s. It was prominent in Bangladesh, Brazil and many Asian countries for the upliftment of the poor.[32]

Grameen Bank[33] has introduced a new concept in microcredit delivery. It has started a banking approach in place of a cooperative approach. Grameen's determination to reform money-lending practices to the poor was successful.[34] Starting its journey from 1976 onwards, the Grameen Bank had lent microcredit loans to 86 per cent of villages in Bangladesh with repayment rate being about 99 per cent of which 97 per cent were women as of May 2006.[35]

Microfinance is used in many developing countries in the world as a key strategy for poverty reduction. Since the late 1980s, the Fiji Government has committed resources in developing microfinance services through the National Centre for Small and Micro Enterprise Development. Other services and lending schemes, particularly for the poor sections, are provided through various Ministries, NGOs and religious organisations.[36]

Following the success of microfinance in a number of developing countries, the Nigerian financial sector in 1990s appears to have developed a penchant for embracing the new trend of MFIs.[37] Microfinance in Argentina presents a puzzle. The rural microfinance organisations have tried to adopt the lessons of urban microfinance to manage the risks and control the costs of the supply of financial services in rural areas. Two factors help explain this. First, the old paradigm still reigns in and second, high wages and sparse populations in South Africa and Argentina raise the cost of small rural loans. Much of the success of rural microfinance in Asia depends on low wages and dense populations.[38] In the year 1986, the World Bank prepared a strategy for low-income housing in developing countries. This work grew out of the Bank's efforts to support the urban poor through an extensive housing assistance programme.[39]

The growth of microfinance in India has also to be seen in the light of financial sector reforms in India starting from 1991 and the global emphasis on commercialization of the sector. The financial sector reforms in India have focused on fostering a market based financial system by increasing competition and improving the quality of financial services.[40] Microfinance has been present in India in one form or another since the 1970s and is now widely accepted as an effective poverty alleviation strategy. Over the last five years, the microfinance industry has achieved significant growth in part due to the participation of commercial banks. Despite this growth, the poverty situation in India continues to be challenging.[41] Rastriya Mahila Kosh (RMK) was set up under the aegis of the Department of Women and Child Development in March 1993 and took up provision of microfinance with particular focus on the women groups.[42]

There is, however, a surge in interest currently among both the Microfinance Institutions (MFIs) and banks to extend micro lending to urban areas. The apprehension about working among the 'transient' urban population[43] groups seems to have given way to optimism about the robust economics of intermediation in the highly densely populated towns and cities. Microfinancial intermediaries are hopeful about achieving 'greater efficiencies by serving heterogeneous urban customers'. While in many cases, this interest has been translated as extension of rural methodologies to the urban-scape, in many others, new and different approaches and products have been developed specifically for the urban poor. The increasing presence of Non-Banking Financial Institutions (NBFCs) in the urban space is an important aspect to take notice of.[44]

Microfinance, which is estimated to be a Rs. 60,000 crore market in India, is growing, with a number of private equities and venture capital firms training their attention at and a few top private banks taking special interest.[45] Life Insurance Corporation of India has been trying to organise all the Non-Governmental Organisations (NGOs), SHGs and other microfinance institutions associated with it to concentrate on the Below Poverty Line (BPL) segment in the cities. It has identified a large untapped customer base in urban segments such as sweepers, vegetable vendors, rickshaw and bus drivers, conductors, labour groups, dhobi and so on.[46] Max New York Life has also developed similar micro insurance product called 'Easy-term Policy'.[47] A Task Force on microfinance recognised in 1999 that microfinance is much more than microcredit, stating it as "Provision of thrift, credit and other financial services and products of very small amounts to the poor in rural, semi-urban and/or urban areas for enabling them to raise their income levels and improve living standards." The SHG promoters emphasise that mobilising savings is the first building block of financial services.[48]

Although the branch network of the formal financial institutions expanded rapidly beginning in the early 1970s, a large segment of the population remained outside the banking fold, especially for its credit requirements. This led to the search for alternative policies and mechanisms for reaching out to the poor to satisfy their felt needs. In this context, microfinance interventions were recognised all over the world as an effective tool that could raise incomes, contribute to individual and household security and change social relations for the better. Though there are different models for purveying microfinance, the SHG-Bank Linkage Programme has emerged as the major microfinance programme in the country. Commercial banks, Regional Rural Banks (RRBs) and co-operative banks are implementing it.[49] Since 2000, in this context, the ADB has been taking initiatives in the region for eradicating poverty.

The SHG-Bank Linkage Programme was started as an Action Research Project in 1989, which was the offshoot of a NABARD initiative during 1987 through Mysore Resettlement and Development Agency (MYRADA) for experimenting Credit Management Groups. In the same year the Ministry of Rural Development provided Professional Assistance for Development Action (PRADAN) with support to establish SHGs. The experiences of these early efforts led to the approval of a pilot project by NABARD in 1992. The pilot project was designed as a partnership model between three agencies, *viz.*, the SHGs, banks and NGOs. A working group reviewed this in 1995 and this review led to the evolution of a streamlined set of RBI approved guidelines to enable SHGs to open bank accounts.[50] A World Bank report suggests that 95 per cent of the members of SHGs do not default in repayment and the efforts of these SHGs need to be lauded.[51]

The aspect of microfinance that has contributed to its success is its 'credit-plus' approach.[52] The success and sustainability of microfinance programmes has in fact depended upon, and has fostered, these aspects.[53] It is claimed that this new paradigm of unsecured small scale financial service provision helps poor people take advantage of economic opportunities, expand their income, smoothen their consumption requirement, reduce vulnerability and also empower them.[54]

Urban Microfinance certainly needs a different approach than rural operations. The process and methodology should be built on the basis of client's needs and preferences. Socio-economic backgrounds of urban poor people are different in various aspects than their rural counterparts. Apart from the problem of rapid urbanization, there is a huge need to generate livelihood opportunities for migrant population from rural areas.[55] The culturally heterogeneous urban poor, some of whom are deprived of even the meagre income for daily existence to begin with cannot be expected to bear even a fraction of the solidarity costs. All those engaged in labour of some kind (domestic servants, taxi drivers, hawkers, rickshaw pullers etc.) are away from the place of residence for most of the day making regular communication and group meetings impossible. Weak social linkage among the urban poor also diminishes any kind of group effort that may earn them credit on support of joint liability and mutual trust.[56]

In reference to urban areas, Urban Credit Society (UCS) is a semi-autonomous self-help institution for saving and borrowing. It is registered under the Cooperative Societies Act. Every UCS is virtually free to advise its own policy and arrange its own affairs, as long as it keeps the interest rates on savings and loans within the limits prescribed by the RBI.[57] It was first initiated in Sangli, a sugar belt district of Maharashtra. The Satin, one of the MFIs working in Delhi estimated that the total population of Delhi and the National Capital Region (NCR) is at 20 million. The number of people living below US $2 per day is approximately, two million.[58]

In the year 2003, the International Environmental Technology Centre (IETC) of the UNEP concentrated its focus on the microfinance in the Urban Environmental Development Perspective under the forum of Urban Environment

Management.[59] A national workshop on "Urban Microfinance in India: Looking Ahead" was organised by the Friends of Women's World Banking (India), Ahmedabad during 21-22 January 2008. The workshop was intended for knowledge building and sharing in relation to the urban poor. A plethora of significant case studies in urban microfinance have been enumerated under the title "Reaching the other 100 Million Poor in India" by the Centre for Microfinance at the Institute for Financial Management and Research, Chennai.

To sum up, it is understood that among several approaches of microfinance, the group approach is familiar in India. The group, basically, is known as Self-Help Group (SHG). It has become a regular component of Indian financial system since 1996. It is small, informal and homogeneous group of not more than 20 members. The advantages of the SHGs can be seen from economic, social, environmental and technological point of view. The success of microfinance depends on the attitude, commitment and sincerity of the group members. The basic objective of the SHG-Bank Linkage programme by the NABARD is to evolve supplementary strategy for meeting the credit needs of the poor by combining informal sector credit system with formal credit institutions. In 2008, the Committee on Financial Inclusion has recommended amendment to NABARD Act to enable it to provide microfinance services to the urban poor. Among the three models of NABARD, Model-II is popular in its operation. In understanding the process of microfinance in reference to urban areas, the review of literature has a greater role not only to build up arguments but also to venture further. Grameen Bank of Bangladesh has introduced a new concept in microcredit delivery with a banking approach in place of a cooperative approach. Microfinance is used in many developing countries in the world as a key strategy for poverty reduction. The growth of microfinance in India has also to be seen in the light of financial sector reforms in India starting from 1991 and the global emphasis on commercialisation of the sector. The aspect of microfinance that has contributed to its success is its 'credit-plus' approach. It is claimed that this new paradigm of unsecured small scale financial service provision helps poor people take advantage of economic opportunities, expand their income, smoothen their consumption requirement, reduce vulnerability and also empower them. Urban Microfinance certainly needs a different approach than rural operations. The process and methodology should be built on the basis of client's needs and preferences.

NOTES AND REFERENCES

1. P. Das and P. Satish (2000): 'Microfinance—Present Scenario and Future Outlook'. *BIRD's Eye View*, March, pp. 13-22.
2. In this model people form groups of three to eight persons on the condition that each of them would be assuming financial responsibility for the other members of the group (e.g., Grameen Bank of Bangladesh, Banco Sol in Bolivia, Latin America).
3. The group approach delegates the entire financial process to the group rather than the financial institutions (e.g., Self-Help Groups—Bank Linkage Programme in India).
4. Credit given directly to the individuals i.e. loan appraisal, loan disbursement, loan repayment as well as saving collections are done in an individual basis (e.g., Indonesia).
5. To an extent, this is an expansion of group approach, where the basic financial necessities of the poor especially the women are met through the community banking system (e.g., Latin America, Africa and Central Asia).
6. Credit unions and cooperatives are member-owned organizations providing credit and other financial services to their members (e.g., Sri Lanka).
7. P. Satish (2005): 'Mainstreaming of Indian Microfinance.' *Economic and Political Weekly*, Vol. XL, No. 17, pp. 1731-32.
8. "The Self-Help Groups are mostly informal groups whose members have a common perception of need and impulse towards collective action. These groups promote savings among members and use the pooled resources to meet the emergent needs of their members, including consumption needs. Sometimes, the generated internal savings are supplemented by external resources loaned by the financial institutions. The SHGs are thus able to provide banking services to their members. These services may not be sophisticated but are cost-effective, simple, flexible, accessible to their members and above all without any defaults in repayments of loans" (Satish, 2001:410). According to the definition given by the NABARD (1992),

SHG is a homogeneous group of rural poor voluntarily formed to save whatever amount they can conveniently save out of their earnings and mutually to be lent to the members for meeting their productive and emergent credit needs.

9. M.L. Gupta and N. Gupta (2006): 'Economic Empowerment of Women through SHGs'. *Kurukshetra,* Vol. 54, No. 4, p. 23.
10. B.D. Prasad and S. Haranath (2004): 'Micro Credit through Self Help Groups: A Strategy in Poverty Alleviation'. In: *Census 2001 and Human Development in India,* (eds.) G. Ramachandrudu and M.P. Rao. New Delhi: Serials Publications, p. 462.
11. In April 1996, RBI advised the banks that lending to the SHGs should be considered as an additional segment under priority sector advances and integrated with mainstream operation.
12. Size of the group should not be more than 20 members, because the group will then have to be legally registered under the Societies Registration Act, 1860.
13. R. Dasgupta (2001): 'An Informal Journey through Self-Help Groups'. *Indian Journal of Agricultural Economics,* Vol. 56, No. 3, pp. 375-76.
14. Credibility refers to the genuineness of demand for credit, credit handling capacity of the members, repayment behaviour within the group, the accounting system and maintenance of the records (Dasgupta, 2001:376).
15. K. Vatta (2003): 'Microfinance and Poverty Alleviation'. *Economic and Political Weekly,* Vol. 38, No. 5, pp. 432-33.
16. *Ibid.* p. 433.
17. R. Dasgupta (2001): 'An Informal Journey through Self-Help Groups'. *Indian Journal of Agricultural Economics,* Vol. 56, No. 3, p. 377.
18. 'Capital' is in economic terms, the money, machinery and plant needed to produce goods. In Sociology, it is often reified to represent a social force in its own right, with its own class interest. Capital is therefore, supposed to operate in predictable ways which often produce exploitation as well as great wealth (Lawson and Garrod, 2003: 26). 'Cultural capital' refers to those desired competences, such as forms of language and expression and valued social skills, which the middle classes are able to confer on their children, together with economic capital. The concept was introduced by Bourdieu (*Ibid.* p. 59). Whereas, 'social capital' refers to the existence of established and well-integrated family and community networks, which act as a support mechanism in times of difficulty. The presence of such capital leads to feelings of security. The absence of social capital is a crucial component of social disorganization (*Ibid.* p. 253). As social capital refers to the aspects of the social structure that are of value to social actors as resources that can be mobilized in pursuit of their interests, social capital is not located in actors themselves (as with human capital) or in any physical implements of production (as with

physical capital). Instead, it is located in the relationships and personal networks among social actors (Karner, 2000: 2638).

19. National Bank for Agriculture and Rural Development (2008): *Report on the Committee of Financial Inclusion.* Mumbai: NABARD, p. 77 (*www.nabard.org/pdf/report_financial/Full%20Report.pdf*).
20. S. Mehrotra and S. Mathur (2006): 'Growth of Institutional Credit'. *Kurukshetra,* Vol. 54, No. 11, p. 22.
21. S.S. Yadav (2006): 'Self-Help Group Movement in Rajasthan: Bright Prospects'. *Kurukshetra,* Vol. 54, No. 11, p. 26.
22. N. Lalith and R. Dayanandan (2005): NABARD and Rural Transformation, New Delhi: Dominant Publishers and Distributers, pp. 1-3.
23. NABARD (2008): p. 77.
24. *Ibid.* p. 83.
25. *Ibid.* p. 77.
26. *Ibid.* p. 80.
27. This is because of the migratory nature of the urban poor, comprising mostly of migrants from rural areas.
28. NABARD (2008): p. 86.
29. "Financial Inclusion means the delivery of banking services and credit at an affordable cost to the vast sections of disadvantaged and low income groups. The various financial services like savings, loans, insurance, payments, remittance facilities and financial counselling and advisory services are offered by the formal financial systems. An open and efficient society is always characterised by the unrestrained access to public goods and services. As banking services are in the nature of public goods, financial inclusion should therefore, be viewed as availability of banking and payment services to the entire population without discrimination of any type" (NABARD, 2008: 33). In other words, Financial Inclusion may be defined as "the process of ensuring access to financial services and timely adequate credit where needed by vulnerable groups such as weaker sections and low-income groups at an affordable cost" (*Ibid.* p. 35). At present, almost 73 per cent of farmer households do not have access to formal credit sources. Hence, "financially excluded households will be defined as those not having any debt to formal credit sources" (*Ibid.* p. 36).
30. N. Sarangi (2007): 'Microfinance and the Rural Poor: A Study of Group-based Credit Programmes in Madhya Pradesh, India'. *Ph.D. Thesis,* New Delhi: Jawaharlal Nehru University, p. 88.
31. R. Dasgupta (2005): 'Microfinance in India: Empirical Evidence, Alternative Models and Policy Imperatives'. *Economic and Political Weekly,* Vol. XL, No. 12, pp. 1235-36.
32. T. Ramesh (2008): 'Microfinance—A Drive to Combat Poverty'. *The Management Accountant,* Vol. 48, No. 11, p. 822.

33. The etymological meaning of the 'Grameen Bank' is the 'Village Bank'. It is understood in reference to Bangladesh, a postcolonial country that has been routed through several political and geographical events. The success of Grameen Bank in Bangladesh has been presented as a role model in the regions of countries facing such challenges. What Prof. Muhammad Yunus has contributed in the success of Grameen Bank is a herculean task. A country is subject to its geography, demographic composition, political and socio-economic conditions. Therefore, the Grameen Bank need not be replicated but be taken a guide and reference to take proper lessons for the future experiments elsewhere.
34. Md. S.H. Choudhury (2000): 'On Sustainable Microfinance Operations', In: *Microfinance: Emerging Challenges* (eds.) K. Basu and K. Jindal. New Delhi: Tata McGraw-Hill Publishing Company Ltd. pp. 71-72.
35. M. Yunus (2006): 'Grameen Bank at a Glance' August, found at *http://www.grameen-info.org*
36. L. Kinivuwai (2005): 'Developing Micro Finance in Fiji: Challenges and Successes' found at *http://www.engagingcommunities2005.org/abstracts/Kinivuwai-Lucy-final.pdf*
37. F.K. Emeni (2008): 'Micro Finance Institutions (MFIs) in Nigeria: Problems and Prospects: Questionnaire Survey Findings'. *Journal of Financial Management and Analysis*, Vol. 21, No. 1, p. 69.
38. M. Schreiner and H.H. Colombet (2001): 'From Urban to Rural: Lessons for Microfinance from Argentina'. *Development Policy Review*, Vol. 19, No. 3, pp. 339-40.
39. J. Kalarickal and R.M. Buckley (2004): 'Shelter Strategy for the Urban Poor: Idiosyncratic and Successful, but Hardly Mysterious', *World Bank Policy Research Working Paper No. 3427*, 07 October *(http://ssrn.com/abstract=625305)*.
40. A. Mishra (2006): 'Microfinance in India and Millennium Development Goals: Maximising Impact on Poverty', *Discussion Paper for the Workshop on World Bank, Singapore* (September 18), p. 8.
41. 'India Grameen Foundation: Where we work: South Asia' found at *(www.grameenfoundation.org/where_we_work/south_asia/india)*.
42. R.K. Sahoo (2008): 'Microfinance and empowerment of the poor'. In: *Microfinance and Rural Development in India* (eds.) S.K. Das, B.P. Nanda and J. Rath. New Delhi: New Century Publications, p. 58.
43. 'Transient' urban population refers to the people who stay for the short duration. They are the temporary visitors from rural areas to the urban areas in search of the livelihood. Basically, they are workers who provide services to the growth and development of the city. They are also sometimes referred to as the floating population.
44. Friends of Women's World Banking (India) (2008): National Workshop on '*Urban Microfinance in India: Looking Ahead*' 21-22

January. Ahmedabad, found at *www.solutionexchange-un.net.in/mf/comm_update/res-12-070108-14.doc.*
45. K. Anand (2008): 'I-banks lose Flavour, IIM Students eye Micro-fin', *The Economic Times,* New Delhi, 24 September, p. 7.
46. 'LIC targets urban poor for micro-insurance products' found at *http://proquest.umi.com/pqdweb.*
47. 'Max NY Life plans micro policies for urban market' found at *http://proquest.umi.com/pqdweb.*
48. 'Microfinance Matters-The Future of Microfinance in India' found at *www.uncdf.org/mfmatters.*
49. Reserve Bank of India (RBI) (2007-08): *Annual Report, 2007-08,* Mumbai: RBI found at *http://www.rbi.org.in/SCRIPTs/Annualreport.aspx.*
50. NABARD (2008): p. 77
51. http://www.chillibreeze.com/articles/Urban-poverty.asp
52. The credit-plus approach essentially, integrates adequate and timely credit into larger developmental process such as community organising, leadership training, entrepreneurship management, financial management, etc. (UNEP, 2005: 4-5).
53. United Nations Environment Programme (UNEP) (2003): 'Microfinance in the Urban Environmental Development Perspective', International Environmental Technology Center, p. 4, found at *www.unep.or.jp/ietc/focus/Microfinance-interlinkages.doc*
54. Asian Development Bank (ADB) (2004): 'Special Theme: The Changing face of the Microfinance Industry', *Annual Report,* Manila: ADB, found at *www.adb.org/documents/reports/annual_report/2004/special-theme.pdf*
55. V. Kumar (2007): 'From Our Desk', *Microfinance Focus,* Vol. 2, No. 1, p.3 foundat*http://www.karmayog.org/redirect/strred.asp?docId=10337*
56. V. Pandey (2007): 'Urban Microfinance—Efforts towards a Lasting Impact', *Microfinance Focus,* Vol. 2, No. 1, p. 6 found at *http://www.karmayog.org/redirect/strred.asp?docId=10337*
57. F.A.J. Bouman (1989): *'Small, Short and Unsecured: Informal Rural Finance in India'*. Delhi: Oxford University Press, p. 44.
58. *'Reaching the Other 100 Million Poor in India'* (2006): Centre for Micro Finance, India, found at found at *http://www.microfinancegateway.org/files/38966_file_20.pdf*
59. UNEP (2003): p. 4.

3

Personality of the Area, Research Methodology and Database

The present chapter incorporates the personality of the area that includes peopling process and transformation of villages through the passage of time. It tries to highlight different objectives of the study. It has also discussed the research methodology, the data, process of collection and the area of the study. The chapter entails the role and composition of the interview schedule, sampling technique and sample size. The emphasis is given to the process of data analysis and the statistical tools used for analysis. The chapter also enumerates limitations of the present study.

Personality of the Area

Delhi is derived from *Hindi* word *'Dehli'* meaning 'threshold'. This is based on the geographical location of Delhi. It lies on the northern most extension of Aravali ranges in the south and close to the Himalayan foothills in the north. This has contributed in placing it at the strategic position in terms of the conventional defence and warfare. Delhi is the largest metropolis of India, with a population of 13.85 million and a federally administered union territory officially known as the National Capital Territory of Delhi (NCT). Delhi[1] is located at 28°37'N to 28°61'N and 77°14'E to 77°23'E. It borders the Indian States of Uttar Pradesh on East and Haryana on West, North and South. Located on the banks of river Yamuna in northern

India, Delhi emerged as a major political, cultural and commercial city along the trade routes between northwest India and the Indo-Gangetic plains. Owing to the immigration of people from across the country, Delhi has grown into a cosmopolitan city. Its rapid development and urbanisation, coupled with the relatively high average income of its population, has transformed the city. Today, Delhi is a major cultural, political, and commercial centre of India.

Table 3.1: Demographic Profile (Census 2001) of Delhi

Parameters		*Total*	*Rural*	*Urban*
Area (sq .km)		1,483	558	925
Total Household		27,33,383	1,79,804	25,53,579
Population	Total	1,38,50,507	9,44,727	1,29,05,780
	Male	76,07,234	5,22,087	70,85,147
	Female	62,43,273	4,22,640	58,20,633
Density (per sq.km)		9,340	1,693	13,952
Population Growth (1991-2001)*		47.02	-0.45	52.34
Sex Ratio		821	810	822
Child Sex Ratio (0-6 yrs.)		868	850	870
Literacy Rate (7 yr. & above)	Total	81.67	78.05	81.93
	Male	87.33	86.60	87.39
	Female	74.67	67.39	75.22
Work Participation Rate	Total	32.82	31.87	32.89
	Male	52.06	49.42	52.25
	Female	9.37	10.18	9.31
Households Having Banking Services#		13,02,645 (47.66)	78,892 (43.88)	12,23,758 (47.92)

Source: Census of India (2001): Primary Census Abstract, Series-8, Delhi.
*Census of India (1991): District Census Handbook, Series-31, Delhi, p. xvii.
Census of India, 2001: H Series: India, pp.499-500.

The National Capital Territory of Delhi is spread over an area of 1,483 sq. km, of which 558 sq. km is designated rural and 925 sq. km urban. Delhi has a maximum length of 51.9 km from north to south and the maximum width of 48.48 km from east to west. There are three local bodies (statutory towns) *viz.*, New Delhi Municipal Council (42.7 sq. km), Delhi Cantonment Board (43 sq. km) and Delhi Municipal Corporation (area is

1,397.3 sq. km).[2] According to the Census of India 2001, the population of Delhi was 13.85 million, which includes 7.61 million males and 6.24 million females. Pronounced urban characteristics of the population can be seen by the fact that 93.6 per cent population of Delhi is residing in urban areas.[3] The corresponding population density[4] was 9,340 persons per sq. with sex ratio[5] of 821 and child sex ratio of 868, literacy rate[6] of 81.67 per cent and work participation rate[7] of 32.82. The population growth in the decade 1991-2001 was 47 per cent. There were 47.66 per cent of households[8] having banking services including 43.88 per cent in the rural and 47.92 per cent in the urban areas (see Table 3.1). There are nine districts and 27 tehsils out of which 16 tehsils in Delhi have rural areas (Census of India 2001).

The Peopling Process

The transformation of urban morphology of Delhi has to be understood through the process of peopling in relation to the social composition of the residing population.[9] The peopling process is subject to a series of events over time and space. There is a direct relationship between the peopling process and the events that guided Delhi to its present form. This can be understood better through the help of historical mapping.

During the pre-British period, the population of Delhi was highly mobile in character. It was only a political and cultural centre with the king as its head, and when he lost his power the city lost all its importance and a new one arose at the next political centre.[10] Different strains from all over the world have contributed to the present social composition of Delhi. "The city had absorbed various elements from neighbouring regions and it housed not only the ruling elite and other officials but also a large number of people from different communities: *Kayasths* (court scribes), *Sarrafs* (jewellers), *Mahajans* (moneylenders), brokers, *Pandits* (brahmins), *Jats* (agriculturists), craftsmen, peasants, *Khatris* (traders), poets, artists, and mendicants."[11]

The establishment of the British rule in India has provided Delhi to become an important commercial centre. Further, the declaration of the Imperial Capital of India in 1911 has provided Delhi a new dimension for the real growth of the population. In fact, "the pull exerted by the new city was very strong. It needed the services of thousand labourers and they came in large numbers from neighbouring areas. In addition, there came in the businessmen and also the officials of Imperial Government who were stationed in the former capital in Calcutta. As the city regained its importance politically, commercially and industrially, more and more people flowed in."[12] The migrant population to Delhi in 1921 and 1931 consisted 45 and 48 per cent of the total respectively.[13] Even the recent census reports show no much changes in the migrant population composition, and large part of the composition is contributed by Uttar Pradesh only.[14]

Much of India's urban population comprises migrants from rural areas where 26 per cent of people are below the line of poverty in 2001. "Women along with their children form part of this vast caravan stream heading for the major cities. They do not head to find work but more often to join their husbands who are in search of labour. They are invariably forced to find shelter in squatter settlements because of lack of affordable housing in cities. Such rural dwellers catapulted into an urban milieu are often faced with radically different surroundings to which they have to adapt."[15]

Enclave and Peripheral Villages

Urban villages[16] are different from the rural villages. The villages in the rural areas[17] are considered to be the epicentre of socialisation. The village composition and settlement are based on the principle of caste structure. The social distance is maintained in the village settlement. The organic behaviour and social relations are based on reciprocity. The economy is simple and agrarian along with the line of *jajmani* system.[18] It is much to the process of domestic modes of production.[19] The division of labour is based on the principle of caste system.

The socio-political life in the village is dominated by the superior castes or the dominant castes.[20] The worldview is based on the socio-cultural guidelines. As a whole, the village in the rural India functions as a unit. However, the process of modernisation has influenced the village life in rural India.[21]

Contrary to the rural villages, the villages in the urban space do not provide rigid characters. The social interaction does not have proper landscape. The people are too busy and contribute little for the social unity. The mode of production is dominated by professionalism and inclined towards non-agricultural sector. There are a lot of opportunities for improvement. Multiple avenues are available at the doorstep. The connectivity is high. The villages in the urban areas are advanced. There is self-centric attitude and we-feeling is a rare occurrence. Here, the respect is based on achievement and not by the seniority of age or cultural prescriptions. The space and time management gets priority. The adjudgement quality and decision-making ability is guided by the power of reasoning and explanation. Contribution and sacrifice cost through mint. As a whole, the money matters a lot. Therefore, the socio-cultural life in the urban villages has a limited scope unlike the rural villages.

Table 3.2: Distribution and Total Number of Inhabited Villages in Delhi (Census 2001)

Population	*Total*
10,000 and Above	24
5,000-9,999	26
2,000-4,999	60
1,000-1,999	29
500-999	9
200-499	4
Less than 200	6
Total Inhabited Villages*	158#

Source: Census of India (2001): District Census Handbook of NCT of Delhi, Series-8, Vol.1.

*All the villages are in rural areas of Delhi.

This constitutes 62, 5, 3, 9, 51 and 16 villages in the Districts North West, North, East, West, South West and South Delhi respectively.

Every city displays a set of unique characters. The characters are germinated over the time. The monuments and remnants of structures describe the cultural past. Delhi is described the place of seven cities. Therefore, one can estimate the centuries old traditions and cultural life of Delhi. However, in recent times, "Delhi, the country's capital displays the overcrowding, insanitation, air pollution, unhealthy and hazardous working condition, transport problems, weakening of communities ties and supports, social alienation, and crime, well known to be the tribulation of contemporary towns and cities worldwide, especially the Third-World, including India. These problems are suffered by all citizens and more by the poor."[22]

In Delhi, there were as many as 300 villages (Census, 1961). It is now 165 villages out of which there are 158 inhabited villages[23] (Census, 2001) (see Table 3.2). Apart from these, there are unauthorised colonies. The settlement process and organisation of villages in Delhi is different from the way it is found elsewhere in India. Though the settlement process of villages has been a slow phenomenon, yet it has been subject to the requirements of the time. The spatial expansion of Delhi has been a continuous process. During the kings' period, the expansion was basically for the security and availability of water. As the time grew, Delhi was made capital and there was a large influx of people to Delhi. The expansion of Delhi was, first, to overcome the building need for the administration of governments and the other, to cover up the pressure of accommodation. It caught the pace during British and Independent India, where the activities of the land galvanised towards urban mode of life.

"Delhi is unusual among world's major cities in that it has managed to push out its growing numbers of the poor to the physical fringes."[24] Traditionally, rural areas of the union territory, the Outer Delhi, have been assigned the role of peripheries, fit to accommodate the masses of slum dwellers in poorly developed resettlement colonies and segments of urban middle classes in sprawling residential complexes planned by the Delhi Development Authority (DDA) along with mushrooming unauthorised colonies. New industrial areas have come up accompanied by the proliferation of new slums, slums and slum-like tenements. Outer Delhi, here, is synonymous with metropolitan periphery.[25] In addition, the proliferation of commercial and manufacturing activities, along with the related services which provide a large number of informal job opportunities, has attracted a floating population of male migrant workers whose residential integration remains extremely precarious.[26]

The concepts of Enclave and Peripheral[27] Villages are very much subjective. The Enclave Villages display urban characteristics as they are surrounded completely by the urban elements and amenities. On the contrary, the Peripheral Villages are of rural in nature. Yet, these villages provide some elements of urbanism, as there is a continuous interaction between the Peripheral Villages with the urban centres of Delhi.

The settlement process in Delhi is never uniformed. There are unauthorised colonies. The people who migrated to the city in search of labour have contributed to the growth of unauthorised colonies. The inhabitants of these colonies are from diverse socio-religious backgrounds. Now, these colonies are influenced and surrounded by the urban way of life. The need of microfinance, in this context, assumes importance.

People, in these areas, have common problems like poverty, malnutrition, unemployment, domestic quarrels, etc. There are needy people. My exposure to all these villages reiterates that there is a demand for the microfinancial activities. Therefore, the present book tries to understand the role of microfinance in the context of unauthorised colonies, Enclave Villages and the Peripheral Villages. As for the requirement of the study, the unauthorised colonies[28] and the urban Villages are clubbed together as Enclave Villages, as they provide urban characters in comparison to the Peripheral Villages.

Research Methodology

Social research is based on logic and empirical observation.[29] According to Charles C. Ragin,[30] "Social research involves the interaction between ideas and evidence. Ideas help social researchers make sense of evidence, and researchers use evidence to extend, revise and test ideas." Social research thus "attempts to create or validate theories through data collection and data analysis. Its goal is exploration, description and explanation. It should never lead or be mistaken with philosophy or belief. Social research aims to find social pattern of regularity in social life and usually deals with social groups (aggregates of individuals), not individuals themselves."[31] The research methodology has been adopted for assessing the impact of microfinance as a tool for understanding the life of people in Delhi. The research methodology includes the present objectives, the selection of the study area, data collection process, building and testing of interview schedule, sample size and implementation of sampling techniques and the statistical tools employed to analyses and present the data.

Research Objectives

The objectives of the present study are (i) to analyse the pattern of socio-demographic and educational status of the SHG members, (ii) to investigate the economic profile of the SHG members, (iii) to evaluate the impact assessment of microfinance through credit and asset structure, (iv) to measure the role of NGOs in implementation of microfinance, and (v) to augment the strategy for better implementation of microfinance.

Process of Data Collection

Field survey[32] seems to be an ideal method of data collection. In social sciences, survey is a method of data collection, in which information is gathered through the interaction with the subject.[33] The process of interaction may be participatory in nature.[34] The interaction process may be formal or informal,[35] oral or written[36] with structured, semi-structured or unstructured interview schedule. The present volume incorporates both primary and secondary data.[37] Primary data have been collected by way of floating interview schedule[38] to collect the information from the respondents[39] who are the members[40] of SHGs in the Enclave and Peripheral villages of Delhi. The survey was conducted by visiting the SHG members with the NGO staff and local people (Photograph 3.1). Several interviews, group discussions and field observations were conducted. The field survey was conducted in between the months of September and November 2008. All the relevant data and opinions sought from this source are embodied into this volume. As far as secondary data are concerned, they are imparted from SHGs records, NGOs records, books, journals, unpublished reports, internet sources, etc. In addition to this, pertinent interactions have been held with concerned staff of Model Rural Youth Development Organisation (MRYDO) (Photograph 3.2) to understand microfinance process, cross check the field data and to collect the information about various kinds of activities extended by the NGOs for the functioning of the SHGs and uplifting the weaker sections in general and women in particular.

Photograph 3.1: NGO Staff and SHG Members with the Researcher at Mahavir Vihar Colony (Kanjhawala), Delhi

Photograph 3.2: Office of the MRYDO, Najafgarh, Delhi

Interview Schedule

Keeping in mind the objectives of the present volume, it was decided to use a schedule[41] as a fieldwork tool, which would supplement the interview process for data collection (Photograph 3.3). A semi-structured interview schedule (see Appendix-1) was designed, which contained series of closed and open-ended questions. In fact, in the interview schedule, data could be said to be collected in two levels. In the first level, information of the household was collected. This included age, sex, marital status, occupation, and relationship to the head of the household. At the second level, information was drawn from women members relating to SHG information, annual income-expenditure pattern of SHG member, impact of joining SHG, level of satisfaction of running the group and the role of NGOs in the development of SHGs, etc.

Criteria for Grouping the Sample Village

The area of the present study belongs to primarily, the South-West District, West District and North West-District of Delhi.

The women members of SHGs interviewed by the researcher belong to 22 villages. This is presented in Table 3.3. All the villages/colonies except Mahabir Vihar and Laxmanpuri belong to the Najafgarh Tehsil of South-West District. The village/colony Mahabir Vihar belongs to the Tehsil Saraswati Vihar under the jurisdiction of North-West District of Delhi. The village Laxmanpuri belongs to the Tehsil Rajouri Garden, West District of Delhi. As described earlier, the classification of villages/colonies[42] is based on their location and discourse with the city of Delhi into Enclave Villages and Peripheral Villages (see Fig. 3.1). The first category of villages (*i.e.,* Enclave Villages) is within the urban fold and includes villages along with unauthorised colonies and the second category of villages (*i.e.,* Peripheral Villages) is on the way to be urbanised. In both the context, the relevance of microfinance assumes dominance for the fact that the poor are everywhere and the attitude to grow and develop is common to all. Given the circumstances, the members would do better.

Photograph 3.3: Interviewing a Senior SHG Member in the Village Bijwasan, Delhi

Table 3.3: Sample Size of SHGs and their Members (Respondents)

Typology	*Villages/Colonies*	*Existing SHGs*[#]	*SHGs (No.) Consulted*	*%age to Total SHGs*	*No. of Respondents* Prominent*
Enclave Villages	1. Raghubir Block (Prem Nagar)	12	10	83.33	20
	2. Roshan Garden	2	1	50.00	2
	3. Dharampura	18	15	83.33	30
	4. Surakh Pur Road	3	3	100.00	6
	5. Roshanpura	2	2	100.00	4
	6. Shiv Enclave	3	3	100.00	6
	7. Bijwasan	7	6	85.71	12
	8. Nangli Sakrawati	6	6	100.00	12
	9. Kapashera	2	2	100.00	4
	10. Laxmanpuri	4	4	100.00	8
	Total	**59**	**52**	**88.14**	**104**
Peripheral Villages	11. Mahavir Vihar	10	9	90.00	19
	12. Dichaun	1	1	100.00	2
	13. Surakh Pur	2	2	100.00	5
	14. Jharoda	7	7	100.00	14
	15. Surera	2	2	100.00	4
	16. Pindwala	4	3	75.00	6
	17. Hasan Pur	6	6	100.00	9
	18. Rewla Kham Pur	7	7	100.00	14
	19. Kair	8	7	87.50	14
	20. Baqar Garh	8	7	87.50	14
	21. Qazi Pur	3	3	100.00	6
	22. Khera Dabar	4	4	100.00	8
	Total	**62**	**58**	**93.55**	**115**
Grand Total		**121**	**110**	**90.91**	**219**

[#] All the SHGs were considered for the detailed study except 11 SHGs due to non-availability of members.
* Women members of SHGs.

Sampling Techniques and Sample Size

A three-tier system has been employed to collect data: firstly, the selection of villages and colonies; secondly, the selection of SHGs; and thirdly, selection of group members (Photograph 3.4). The sampling techniques adopted in this context are the judgement

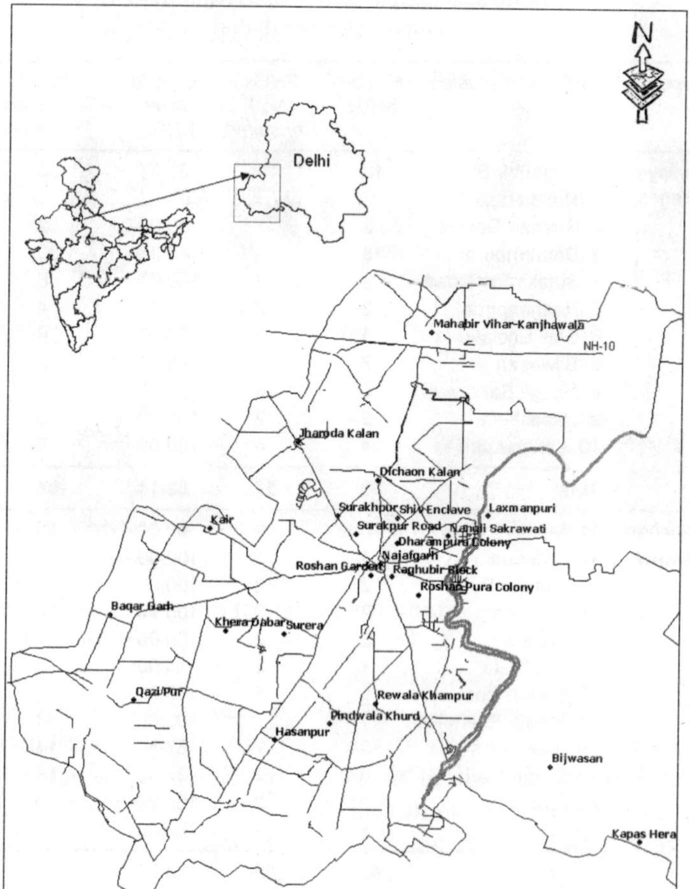

Fig. 3.1: Sample Villages/Colonies in Najafgarh Area, Delhi, Year 2008-2009

sampling,[43] the convenience sampling[44] and the snowball sampling[45] to follow up the above three stages respectively. The flow chart of sample design has been depicted in Fig. 3.2.

Selection of Villages and Colonies

The NGO called MRYDO, Najafgarh, Delhi was contacted to support the researcher in order to carry out the field survey

Photograph 3.4: Author with the SHG Members at Dharampura, Delhi

on the SHGs to understand the nature of microfinance in Delhi region. The SHGs were formed by the intermediation of this NGO in collaboration with the NABARD, Delhi Commission for Women (DCW), RMK and Gender Resource Centre (GRC). Thus the whole sketch of selecting villages and settlements was done by the MRYDO where the SHGs were active by adopting judgement sampling. Altogether 22 villages/colonies were visited by the researcher for this volume (see Table 3.3).

Selection of Self-Help Groups

The Convenience sampling technique was employed to select the SHGs in the villages. Altogether 110 SHGs (91 per cent) were consulted out of the total 121 existing SHGs. All the existing groups were consulted in the villages/colonies such as Raghubir Block (Prem Nagar), Roshan Garden, Dharampura, Surakh Pur Road, Rosanpura, Shiv Enclave, Bijwasan, Nangli Sakrawati (Photograph 3.5), Kapashera and Laxmanpuri constituting Enclave Villages; and Mahavir Vihar (Kanjhawala), Dichaun, Surakh Pur, Jharoda, Surera, Pindwala, Hasan Pur, Rewla Kham Pur, Kair, Baqar Garh (Photograph 3.6), Qazi Pur and Khera

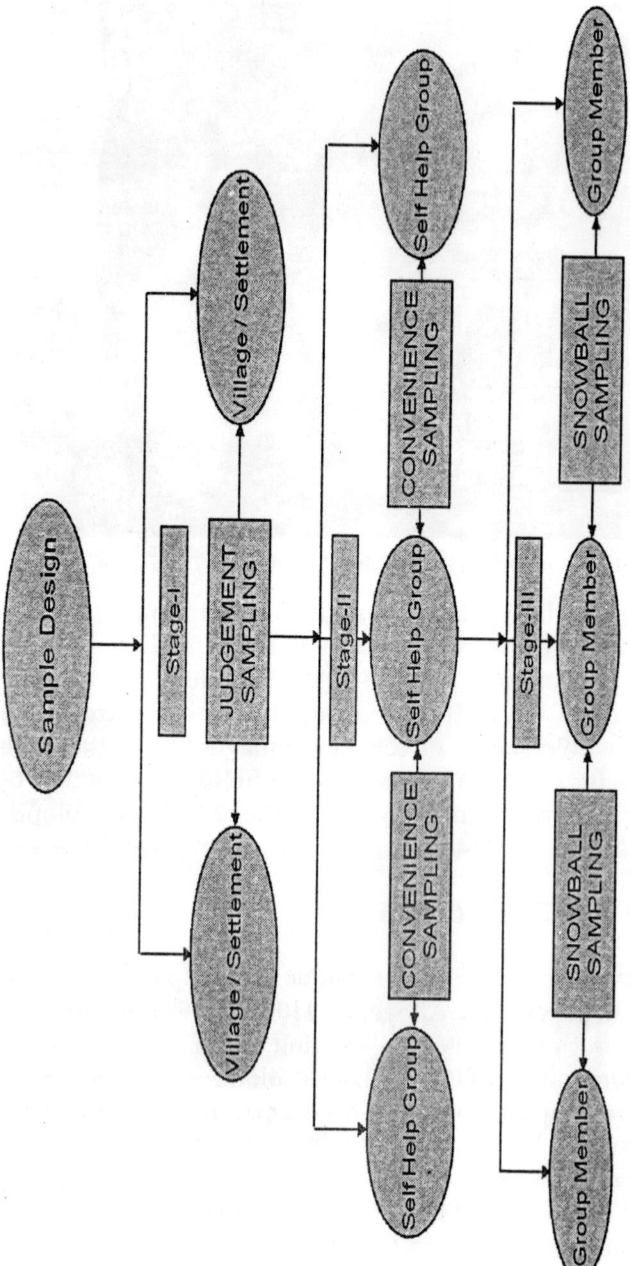

Fig. 3.2: Flow Chart of Sample Design

Photograph 3.5: Author with the SHG Members in Nangli Sakrawati, Delhi

Photograph 3.6: Author interacts with the SHG Members in Baqar Garh Village, Delhi

Dabar constitute Peripheral Villages (see Table 3.3). A total of 52 SHGs (88 per cent) and 58 SHGs (94 per cent) were consulted from the Enclave Villages and Peripheral Villages respectively.

Selection of Group Members

The Snowball sampling technique was employed to select the SHG members. Altogether, 219 group members with 104 and 115 women members from the Enclave Villages and Peripheral Villages were interviewed respectively with minimum of one and maximum of three members from an SHG. In most of the cases, two members were selected from an SHG (see Table 3.3).

Analysis of Data

Data do not, however, 'speak for themselves'. They reveal what the analyst can detect. So when the investigator, attempting to collect this reward, finds himself/herself alone with the dataset and no idea how to proceed, the feeling may be one more of anxiety than of eager anticipation. As with most other aspects of a study, analysis and interpretation of the study should relate to the study objectives and research questions.[46] The phase of data processing includes the plan of analysis as prepared by the researcher. It includes all the process that will facilitate screening, sorting out of the relevant data and then preparing the data for analysis. The most relevant process after the collection of data is its analysis. Once the classification of data is complete, the process of analysis starts. Data analysis is interpretation of available information in a manner to establish cause-effect relationship. The analysis of data constitutes either establishing the truthfulness of preliminary hypothesis or its relation on the basis of collected data.[47] In this phase major activities are carried out such as, data classification, categorisation of sample members, classification and categorisation of answers, opinions or replies into data quantification.

After collecting the primary and secondary information, data are analysed mostly in a descriptive way while the quantitative data are presented in the tables, figures and percentages. Once the data are analysed, their reliability is determined and the report is written embodying the survey findings. Validity and accuracy of survey data are examined through introducing the checks and rechecks. In short, after the collection of data from the field, the data have been analyzed and interpreted. Inferences have been drawn from the interpreted data.

Report writing is a difficult and most arduous part of survey research.[48] In order to ensure the scope of work required to meet the objectives, the study was fully addressed and a tentative outline of the report was first prepared. Various pieces of information collected during the field survey were organized and analyzed for the purpose of report preparation. The analysis covered the detailed assessments of the members such as socio-demographic accounts, year of joining SHG, sources of motivation for joining the SHGs, size of the SHGs, economic profile, credit structure, purpose of credit by members of SHGs, average annual return (AAR), average annual expenditure (AAE), asset structure of SHG members, asset building process of SHG members, impact of joining SHGs.

For computation of the information, (i) Software package has been used, (ii) for the graphs and other analysis, Ms-Excel has been used, (iii) for text and report writing, Ms-Word has been used, and (iv) for maps and photographs, Microsoft Photo Editor and World Wide Web (www) have been used. The quantitative techniques used for the analysis are (i) percentage, (ii) simple average and arithmetic mean, (iii) standard deviation, (iv) coefficient of variation, (v) quartiles, (vi) graphical representation, etc.

Statistical Tools Employed

Analysis of the primary data have been done by employing various statistical tools including percentage, simple average and arithmetic mean, standard deviation, coefficient of variation, quartiles, graphs, etc. by the help of Microsoft Excel Spreadsheet.

Percentage

A percentage is proportion multiplied by 100.

Arithmetic Mean

It is the average value for a series of numbers. It is defined as the sum of individual observations divided the total number of observations.

Standard Deviation

It is the square root of the mean amount of deviation of each score from its own mean or the root of mean deviation.

Coefficient of Variation

Ratio scales are useful in social science research when an investigator is interested in the variability of a sample on one characteristic as compared with another. This is expressed in percentage. It is the standard deviation divided by mean and multiplied by 100.

Quartiles

This divides up a distribution into four parts. Thus the first quartile (Q_1) is the same as P_{25} and the third quartile (Q_3) is the same as P_{75}. The Q_2 is same as 50th percentile (P_{50}).

Graphs

The graph represents visual description of the sample with respect to stated major. It provides more information than the data tables. The levelling of graph is important, because they convey information to self and to others. The axes should be levelled so that the nature of the graph is self-evident.[49] In the present study, bar graphs, line graphs and pie charts have been used. A pie chart is a circle divided into wedges for which the central angle is proportional to the relative frequency of the graph categories.[50]

Calculation of Distance Index

The steps involved in the construction of distance index[51] for seven indicators are appended below:

Step 1: Making the Indicator Scale Free

(i) Computation of the mean for each indicator. For the jth indicator, the mean X_j^* would be $\Sigma X_{ij}/N$ where X_{ij} is the value of the ith village for j^{th} indicator and i=1,2,....N. N is the number of villages, which is 22 (Enclave Villages:10 and Peripheral Villages: 12) in the present case for each indicator.

(ii) Division of each observation of the indicator (X_{ij}) by the respective mean (X_j^*). We thus obtain X_{ij}/X_j^*. These may be called the scale free values of the indicators.

Step 2: Adding up the Scale Free Values of the jth Indicator for each Village

$$D_j = \Sigma(X_{ij}/X_j^*);\ j = 1, 2, \ldots.\ 7.$$

Finally, the distance index is $D_j^* = D_j/k$, where k is the total number of indicators, which is 7, as noted above.

The Index shows that higher the value for a village the higher the village will be in a disadvantageous position. The lower the values the more connected the village to the important destinations. Name and approximate distance (in km.) of village/colony from important destinations is shown in Appendix 2.

Limitations of the Study

The following are the limitations of the present volume such as:

- The inferences drawn are based on primary data from a small sample using a three tier sampling techniques such as the judgement, convenience and snowball.
- The study area is only stipulated to few villages in the region of Delhi where the SHGs are found.
- The gestation period of the present study is about four months (September to December 2008); the results might vary when compared with other long gestation studies with larger sample size.

- The theoretical presentations of the primary data were according to the researcher's view; they might be different from the views of others.

To sum up, social research is based on logic and empirical observations. Social research involves the interaction between ideas and evidence. Ideas help social researchers make sense of evidence, and researchers use evidence to extend, revise and test ideas. Social research thus attempts to create or validate theories through data collection and data analysis, and its goals are exploration, description and explanation. The research methodology has been adopted for assessing the impact of microfinance as a tool for Enclave Villages and Periphery Villages in Delhi. The study has embodied both primary and secondary data. Primary data have been collected by way of canvassing an interview schedule from the respondents who are the women members of the SHGs in Delhi by the help of an NGO called MRYDO. As far as secondary data are concerned they are imparted from SHGs records, NGOs records, books, journals, unpublished reports, internet sources, etc. The primary data were collected mainly from women members of SHGs. The data were collected from 22 villages of South-West, West and North-West Districts of Delhi in between September and November 2008 and consulting 219 women SHG members from 110 Self-Help Groups. Altogether 110 SHGs (90.91 per cent) were consulted out of the total 121 SHGs existing in the villages, which constitute a total of 52 SHGs (88 per cent) and 58 SHGs (94 per cent) from the Enclave Villages and Peripheral Villages respectively.

NOTES AND REFERENCES

1. 'Delhi' found at *http://en.wikipedia.org/wiki/Delhi*.
2. Census of India, 2001: Provisional Population Totals (Paper 2 of 2001 Rural-Urban Distribution of Population) Series 8: Delhi; 'Introduction', *New Delhi Municipal Council Act, 1994,* found at *http://www.ndmc.gov.in/AboutNDMC/NNDMCAct.aspx;*
3. Census of India (2001): *Primary Census Abstract,* Series 8: Delhi, p. xiv.

4. Density of population is measured in terms of number of people per sq. area.
5. According to the Census of India, the sex ratio is defined as the number of females per 1000 males. However, child sex ratio (0-6 years) has been defined as the number of females in age group of 0-6 years per 1000 males in the same age group in the population.
6. As defined by the Census of India, literacy rate of population is the percentage of literates to the total population of age 7 years and above.
7. According to the Census of India, work participation rate is defined as the percentage of total workers (main and marginal) to total population.
8. A 'household' is usually a group of persons who normally live together and take their meals from a common kitchen unless the exigencies of work prevent any of them from doing so. Persons in a household may be related or unrelated or a mix of both. *(Census of India 2001: India,* H Series, p. 77).
9. V. Dupont (2000): 'Mobility Patterns and Economic Strategies of Houseless People in Old Delhi'. In: *Delhi: Urban Space and Human Destinies* (eds.) V. Dupont, E. Tarlo and D. Vidal. New Delhi: Manohar Publishers and Distributors, p. 103.
10. A. Bopegamage (1957): *Delhi: A Study in Urban Sociology*. Bombay: University of Bombay, p. 31.
11. V. Goel (2003): Delhi: *The Emperor's City*. New Delhi: Roli Books, pp. 24-26.
12. A. Bopegamage (1957): pp. 32-33.
13. *Ibid.* p. 33.
14. V. Dupont (2000): pp. 108-9.
15. S. Haider (2000): 'Migrant Women and Urban Experience in a Squatter Settlements'. In: *Urban Space and Human Destinies* (eds.) V. Dupont, E. Tarlo and D. Vidal. New Delhi: Manohar Publishers and Distributors, p. 29.
16. The definition of 'urban unit' adopted by the Census of India implies that a place may have the following criteria such as (i) a minimum population of 5,000; (ii) at least 75 per cent of male working population engaged in non-agricultural pursuits; and a density of population of at least 400 per sq. km. Some villages are treated as urban because they satisfy these criteria and such villages are termed as 'Census Towns' although no notification for their urbanisation has been issued by the State Government and the same continue to figure in revenue records as villages (Census of India, 2001).
17. The basic unit of rural areas is the 'village', which has definite surveyed boundaries. Village is a statutory recognized unit having a definite boundary and separate land records (Census of India, 2001). In the text, the word 'settlement' is used interchangeably for villages. A

settlement is a general term used for a permanent or temporary community in which people live, without being specific as to size, population of importance. The term may include hamlets, villages, towns and cities (http://en.wikipedia.org/w:k:/human_settlement).

18. *Jajmani* system refers to traditional economic interaction in rural India based on the caste tradition (Gould, 2002: 126-27). Each caste in the village at sometime during the year is expected to render a fixed type of services to each other caste (Wiser, 1936: xviii). In return for the various services rendered, there are payments in cash and kind made daily, monthly, biyearly, per piecework, and on special occasions, depending on the type of services rendered and in part on the goodwill of *jajman* (*Ibid.* p. xxiv). Within the villages, the patron-client relation is manifested itself mainly in the *jajmani* system (Srinivas, 1987: 11).
19. It refers to the organisation of economic production and consumption primarily in the household found at *http://www.webref.org/anthropology/d/domestic_mode_of_production. htm*
20. Referring to the village Rampura near Mysore city, the concept of the dominant caste is crucial to the understanding of rural social life in most parts of India. "A caste may be said to be 'dominant' when it preponderates numerically over the other castes, and when it also wields preponderant economic and political power. A large and powerful caste group can be more easily dominant if its position in the local caste hierarchy is not too low" (Srinivas, 1955: 18).
21. Modernisation, as of cultural response, involves attributes, which are basically universalistic and evolutionary; they are pan-humanistic, trans-ethnic and non-ideological. Modernisation may in this respect be treated as a kind of 'cultural-universal', not at the level of higher order of culture (Kluckhohn, 1953: 507-09). Modernisation implies a form of cultural change that orthogenetic civilizations have undergone in contact with exogenous cultural systems. But what may be essential to modernisation are the commitment to scientific worldview, the internalisation of humanistic and philosophical viewpoint of science on contemporary problems and not merely the volume of technological advancement (Singh, 1973: p. 61). Srinivas prefers the term westernisation to modernisation (*Ibid.* p. 9). By westernisation, it is understood "the changes brought about in Indian society and culture as a result of over 150 years of British rule, the changes occurring at the levels of technology, institution, ideology and values" (Srinivas, 1962: 55).
22. R. Priya (2006): 'Town Planning, Public Health and Delhi's Urban Poor: A Historical Review'. In: *Urban Studies.* (eds.) S. Patel and K. Dev. New Delhi: Oxford University Press, p. 223.
23. For identification of 'Census Towns' for 2001, the criteria adopted are such as (i) all places with the three statutory towns i.e., New

Delhi Municipal Council, Delhi Cantonment Board and Delhi Municipal Corporation and (ii) all other places which satisfy the following criteria of (a) a minimum population of 5,000, (b) at least 75 per cent of the male working population engaged in non-agricultural pursuits, and (c) a density of population of at least 400 per sq. km. These criteria were applied for all those villages, which were having a population of 4,000 and more as per the 1991 Census. Accordingly 59 villages were treated as census towns for Census 2001. Thus the urban component for N.C.T. of Delhi for Census 2001 comprises 62 towns i.e., 3 statutory towns and 59 census towns. In Delhi, there are 27 Tehsils, which comprise 59 census towns, and 165 villages; for example, there are 2 census towns and 49 villages under Najafgarh Tehsil (Census of India 2001: *Provisional Population Totals*, Series-8, pp. 3-6).

24. J. Ghosh (1994): 'The Expansionist City'. *Frontline*, Chennai, 20 May, p. 110.
25. A. Soni (2006): 'Urban Conquest of Outer Delhi Beneficiaries, Intermediaries and Victims: The Case of Mehrauli Countryside'. In: *Urban Studies*. (eds.) S. Patel and K. Dev. New Delhi: Oxford University Press, p. 295.
26. A.K. Mehra (1991): *The Politics of Urban Redevelopment: A Study of Old Delhi*. New Delhi: Sage Publication, p. 46.
27. According to the Concise Oxford Dictionary (Tenth Edition), 'enclave' means a portion of territory surrounded by a larger territory whose inhabitants are culturally and ethnically distinct. In other words, a group that is different in character from those surrounding it. Whereas, the term 'periphery' refers to the outer limits or edge of an area. Its origin is from the Greek word '*periphereia*' meaning circumference.
28. The unauthorized colonies, *i.e.*, Raghubir Block (Prem Nagar), Roshan Garden, Dharampura, Surakh Pur Road, Roshanpura, Shiv Enclave and Laxmanpuri have been considered as Enclave villages for the present study.
29. According to the Concise Oxford Dictionary, the term 'empirical' observation refers to research that is based on, concerned with, or verifiable by observation or experience rather than theory or pure logic.
30. C.C. Ragin (1994): '*Constructing Social Research: The Unity and Diversity of Method*', California: Pine Forge Press (Sage Publications Company), pp. 55-57.
31. 'Social Research' found at *http://en.wikipedia.org/wiki/Social_research*
32. Field survey is conducted in a specified geographical area where the research is intended to be carried out on a selected population.
33. 'Subject' here is a unit of universe, on which the data is extracted for the purpose of the research study. This term is also used

interchangeably with the terms like ego, respondent, participant, interviewee, group member etc.

34. The participant observer gets involved in the actual daily life of the group, which one studies. The researcher shares in the life and activities of the community observing in the strict sense what is going on around him/her by supplementing this by conversations, interviews and studies of records (Moser, 1969: 168). In other words, in social science research in general and anthropological research in particular, participant observation is a popular method of fieldwork, where the researcher observes keenly the social behaviour of the participants through taking part in the socio-cultural activities of the society. This is one of the laborious and most effective methods of data collection.
35. The process of interaction with the subject is through relaxed and unofficial manner. This is informal.
36. The interaction process is basically spoken rather than written. Language is primarily spoken and secondarily written. The most lively and unbiased interaction for getting into the fact is when it is conducted in an informal and verbal environment. The other form of interaction process is conducted with preparedness through written format with series of open-ended (unstructured) and close-ended (structured) questions.
37. Primary data refers to information collected by the researcher at first hand, whereas information used but not created by the researcher is secondary data. These data include historical and personal documents, books, journals, census reports, newspapers, etc.
38. Interview schedule is an instrument used for the data collection through structured or semi-structured interview with a set of open and close-ended questions. The questions are put systematically and the researcher fills it up by asking the interviewee the set of questions mentioned in the interview schedule. With a close-ended question, the respondents are presented with a set of fixed alternatives from which they have to choose an appropriate answer. Open-ended questions are filled up by the researcher as the respondents react to the questions.
39. Almost all members of the SHGs formed by the intermediation of MRYDO are women. Hence, the members of the functional SHGs consulted/interviewed by me for the present volume on microfinance are women. The NABARD's inclination towards women of SHGs is based on the experience and success of the Grameen Bank of Bangladesh. The experience of Muhammad Yunus suggests that the credit given to women brings about changes faster than when given to men. "A poor woman in the society is totally insecure. She is insecure in her husband's house because he can throw her out any time he wishes. Being poor is tough for everyone, but being a poor woman is toughest of all. When she is given the smallest opportunity,

she struggles extra hard to get out of poverty. Money going through a woman in a household brings more benefits to the family as a whole than money entering the household through a man" (Yunus, 2007: 88).

40. For the present volume on microfinance, the sample constitutes minimum of one member and maximum of three women members from an SHG. In majority of cases, only two women members were interviewed from an SHG.
41. Schedule means interview schedule (See Note 38). There is difference between schedule and questionnaire. The questionnaire should normally be filled by the respondent in his own hand, whereas a schedule is filled by the interviewer who asks questions and records the reply.
42. In the present study, villages constitute the settlements like unauthorised and authorised colonies and villages. The classification of Enclave and Peripheral villages and clubbing the settlements under the present typology is to understand the effect of urban influence on the functioning of SHGs. The typology is purely from the viewpoint of academic perspective. There is no contour line, which divides the villages/colonies into Enclave and Periphery villages. The adjudgement of villages/colonies into these two categories is based on the field survey of the scholar to these settlements, which qualify the characteristics of Enclave and Peripheral villages.
43. A judgement sample is obtained according to the discretion of someone who is familiar with the relevant characteristics of the population. (found at *http://www.socialresearchmethods.net/tutorial/Mugo/tutorial.htm*). Judgement samples are drawn by the researcher to select only such cases that he considers to be typical of the whole lot. The researcher selects different kinds of people who may give different kinds of opinions, reactions and responses. The advantage of judgement samples is that these are speedily administered and are economical (Sharma, 1988: 95-96).
44. There are three main types of non-probability sample, such as the convenience sample, the snowball sample and the quota sample. A convenience sample results when the more convenient elementary units are chosen from a population for observation (found at *http://www.socialresearchmethods.net/tutorial/Mugo/tutorial.htm).* In other words, "a convenience sampling is one that is simply available to the researcher by virtue of its accessibility" (Bryman, 2008: 183).
45. In social science research, snowball sampling is a technique for developing a research sample where existing study subjects recruit future subjects from among their acquaintances. Thus the sample group appears to grow like a rolling snowball. As the sample builds up, enough data is gathered to be useful for research (found at *http:/*

/en.wikipedia.org/wiki/Snowball_sampling). In other words, in this type of sampling, "researchers begin the research with the few respondents who are available to them. They subsequently ask these respondents to recommend any other persons who meet the criteria of the research and who might be willing to participate in the project. If and when such respondents are recommended, the investigators approach them, collect the information required and ask them to recommend other persons who might fit the research design and be willing to be studied. The process is continued until the sample is structured" (Sarantakos, 1994: 139).

46. *www.epidemiolog.net/evolving/DataAnalysis-and-interpretation.pdf*
47. R.M. Sharma (1988): *Research Methods in Social Sciences,* New Delhi: National Book Organisation, pp. 101-02.
48. *Ibid.* p. 102.
49. L.A. Marascuilo and R.C. Serlin (1988): *Statistical Methods for the Social and Behavioural Sciences.* New York: W.H. Freeman and Company, pp. 31-44.
50. *Ibid.* p. 46.
51. N. Sarangi (2007): 'Microfinance and the Rural Poor: A Study of the Group-based credit Programmes in Madhya Pradesh, India'. Ph.D. Thesis, New Delhi: Jawaharlal Nehru University, p. 178.

4

Socio-Demographic and Educational Status of Self-Help Group Members

An SHG is a channel through which microfinance is routed to the poor with a philosophy that it would prove catalytic in helping them pull out of poverty. It is, like a mini bank based on homogeneity, mutual cooperation, collective performance and responsibility. There is a huge unmet demand for microfinance in India. In this chapter, an attempt has been made to analyse and interpret the data on social, demographic and educational status of the sample members. These include the age group of the SHG members, their marital status, educational status, family type, housing and residential ownership, place of birth and migration, year of joining the group, sources of motivation and size of the group. These are some of the vital information about the members, which have some strength on the performance of SHGs. The comparative account on socio-demographic and educational status of the members belonging to the Enclave and Peripheral Villages in Delhi tries to explain the building process of microfinance.

Age Group of Sample Members

Age group of the sample SHG members has been enumerated in Table 4.1. In the sample, there are maximum members in the category of age group of 31-40 years. It is 36.54 per cent and 42.61 per cent and in the Enclave and Peripheral Villages respectively. In the Enclave Villages, the second highest concentration of the members lies in the age group of 21-30 years followed by that of 41-50 years with 29.81 per cent and 18.27 per cent respectively. Contrary to this, in the Peripheral Villages, the second highest concentration of members is drawn from the age group of 41-50 years followed by 21-30 years with 25.22 per cent and 19.13 years respectively. It is important to see that the age group of 51-60 years with a presence of 10.43 per cent and 6.73 per cent in the Peripheral and Enclave Villages respectively, is influential. However, in both type of villages, the concentration of members decreases at the two extremes

Table 4.1: Age Group of the Sample SHG Member

Age Group (in Yr.)	*Enclave Villages*		*Peripheral Villages*		*Total*	
	No.	*%*	*No.*	*%*	*No.*	*%*
< 21	7	6.73	1	0.87	8	3.65
21-30	31	29.81	22	19.13	53	24.20
31-40	38	36.54	49	42.61	87	39.73
41-50	19	18.27	29	25.22	48	21.92
51-60	7	6.73	12	10.43	19	8.68
> 60	2	1.92	2	1.74	4	1.83
Total	**104**	**100.00**	**115**	**100.00**	**219**	**100.00**

Source: Field Survey, 2008.

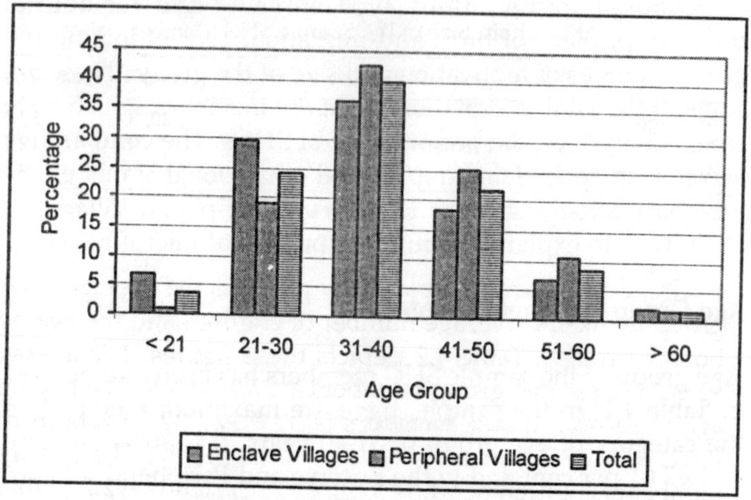

Fig. 4.1: Showing the Age Group of Sample Members

i.e., lower and higher age group categories. But, in the Enclave Villages, there is some impact still at the age group below 21 years with a presence of 6.73 per cent (see Fig. 4.1).

The probable reasons for this kind of pattern may be the following:

(i) In the Enclave Villages, the concentration pattern of members picks up in the lower age groups than the higher age groups with the spurt at the age group 31-40 years. The awareness is faster among the members. The onset of maturity is earlier. This is basically due to the urban mode of life. There is a tendency among the members to face the urban race and challenges.

(ii) In the Peripheral Villages, the progression of life arrives late. The process for building of capacity takes some time. There is no tendency for a sudden rise. The understanding and guidance to the fact of conformity works along the line of examination and scrutiny. This is because of the fact that village community works in the direction of cohesiveness based on socio-cultural experiences.

Table 4.2: Average Age, Average No. of Children and Average Household Size of the Sample SHG Members

Parameters	*Enclave Villages*	*Peripheral Villages*	*Total*
Avg. Age (In Yr.)	35.90	39.50	37.79
Avg. No. of Children per Woman	2.69	2.76	2.73
Avg. Household Size	4.91	4.89	4.90

Source: Field Survey, 2008.

In addition, the sample study presents the average age of group members, average number of children and the average household size. Table 4.2 depicts these figures. The average age of the sample group members is 37.79 years. The average age of sample group members is 35.9 and 39.5 years in the Enclave and Peripheral Villages respectively. The average number of children per the group member stands at 2.73, which is 2.69 and 2.76 in the Enclave and Peripheral Villages respectively. However, the average household size for the sample group members is 4.9 with 4.91 and 4.89 in the Enclave and Peripheral Villages respectively. This relates to the fact that there is no much variation between these two types of settlements. However, the following points may clarify the differences, such as:

(i) In the average age of the sample SHG members, it is found that the Enclave Villages have less young population and the average number of children per woman is less than that of the Peripheral Villages. This implies that awareness among the members is high. Every activity is based on the rational thinking. This is considered in terms of cost evaluation. This is perhaps due to urban way of life.

(ii) In the Peripheral Villages, there are members in the higher age group that is indicative from the average age of sample SHG members. However, they have household size which is almost equal to the Enclave Villages. The priority areas of life have to be planned in advance in both the settlements.

Table 4.3: Marital Status of the Sample SHG Members

Marital Status	*Enclave Villages*		*Peripheral Villages*		*Total*	
	No.	*%*	*No.*	*%*	*No.*	*%*
Unmarried	7	6.73	1	0.87	8	3.65
Married	91	87.5	106	92.17	197	89.95
Divorced	1	0.96	—	—	1	0.46
Widow	5	4.81	8	6.96	13	5.94
Total	104	100.00	115	100.00	219	100.00

Source: Field Survey, 2008.

Marital Status of Sample Members

Table 4.3 shows the marital status of the sample group members. Altogether, 90 per cent group members are married. This is 92.17 per cent for the members in the Peripheral Villages and 87.5 per cent in the Enclave Villages. Unmarried group members are found more in the Enclave Villages (6.73 per cent) than in the Peripheral Villages with only 0.87 per cent in the total sample that recorded 3.65 per cent. There are widows, who are also the part of the SHGs. Their presence is at 4.81 per cent and 6.96 per cent in the Enclave and Peripheral Villages respectively with a total of 5.94 per cent. There are no divorcee members in the Peripheral Villages as it has a rare occurrence in the society. However, the Enclave settlements have just one divorcee (0.96 per cent), who is also currently a member of the SHG (see Fig. 4.2). My interaction with the SHGs entails that the group is found to be very helpful to the needy persons who run their families with financial difficulties. It helps in regular lending to members and its timely recovery from members, though flexibility is not non-existent.

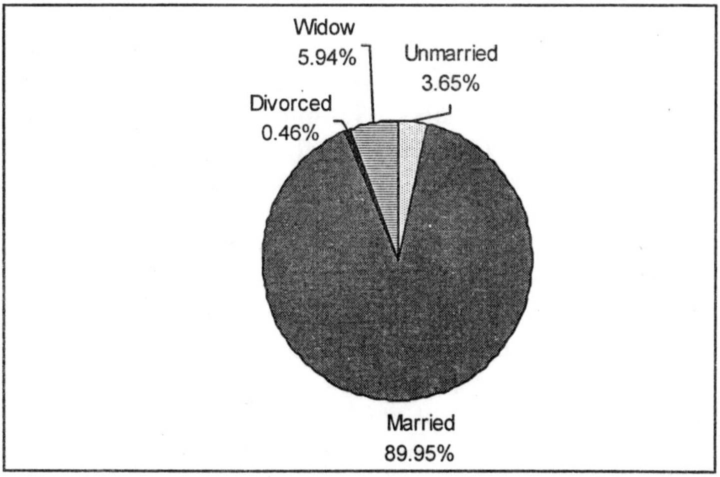

Fig. 4.2: Pie Chart Showing the Marital Status of the Sample SHG Members

The following reasons may be attributed to the distribution pattern in the marital status of group members.

(i) In the Enclave Villages, the SHG acts an open forum where the participation and membership is based on the need. This may arise because there is awareness among the youth. The foresight towards life reaches faster among them than their counterparts in the Peripheral settlements as the former is guided by the faster way of urban life. It seems that there is difficulty in arranging suitable women members for the group. The group cannot make anybody and everybody as its member. Sometimes, the unmarried girls become members, as there is requirement for the membership. They, in fact, help in maintaining the books of account. Therefore, the percentage of unmarried members is higher in the Enclave Villages than in the Peripheral Villages.

(ii) In the Peripheral Villages, the life is comparatively slow. The young mass is dependent on the parents for a longer time. The wants are limited. The young sections are often busy with the village life, which has a lot to do with domestic works like collection of fodder and other related works. The mind towards money and finance has little catch on them. This is perhaps the purview of elderly persons like mother, who has got higher freedom in the domestic financial health of the family. It is she who acts as a manager in the internal matters of the family.

Educational Status of Sample Members

Education is an important wealth for any society because it increases the level of information, and ultimately the knowledge received through formal and informal ways incorporates different dimensions to the human life. Advancement of a society can be estimated through its educational level.[1] The level of education has direct linkage with the efficiency of SHGs. The maintenance of books of accounts, decision-making power and attitude towards group value per se are all controlled by the level of education. Thus, education is the key to improvement in quality of life.

Table 4.4: Educational Status of the Sample SHG Members

Educational Status	*Enclave Villages*		*Peripheral Villages*		*Total*	
	No.	*%*	*No.*	*%*	*No.*	*%*
Illiterates	23	21.15	39	34.78	62	28.31
Primary Level (Upto V)	6	5.77	8	6.96	14	6.39
Middle Class (VI-VIII)	19	18.27	10	8.70	29	13.24
Matriculation (IX-X)	29	27.88	34	29.57	63	28.77
Intermediate (XI-XII)	19	18.27	14	12.17	33	15.07
Above Intermediate & Professional Courses	9	8.65	9	7.83	18	8.22
Total	**104**	**100.00**	**115**	**100.00**	**219**	**100.00**

Source: Field Survey, 2008.

Table 4.4 displays the educational status of the sample group members. There is higher percentage of illiterates in the sample groups of Peripheral Villages (34.78) than of the Enclave Villages (21.15). More group members are at the level of matriculation recording 27.88 and 29.57 per cent in case of Enclave and Peripheral Villages respectively. The cursory look at the table depicts that in case of Enclave Villages there is a jump on the level of education of members from primary to middle level. However, the jump especially for matriculation is very much distinct in the case of Peripheral Villages. Subsequently, the change slows down towards higher education among the members in both the settlements (see Fig. 4.3).

The reasons for this kind of pattern of educational level may be as follows:

(i) In the Enclave Villages, the group members belong to the diverse socio-cultural background. The perception towards life is different. The dropout rates at each level are guided by the economic opportunity, which are basically of short-term in nature. There is occupational shift among the members as percentage of illiterates is low in comparison to the Peripheral Villages, where members hold on to the traditional occupation.

(ii) In the Peripheral Villages, people are bound by a common socio-cultural background. The aims and objective are simple with common perception towards life. There may be two types of views regarding the pattern of education among the group members: firstly, there is no study at all as a result higher illiteracy rate; secondly, if someone intends to study, it is taken without any interruption. Thus, one-third of group members are at the level of matriculation.

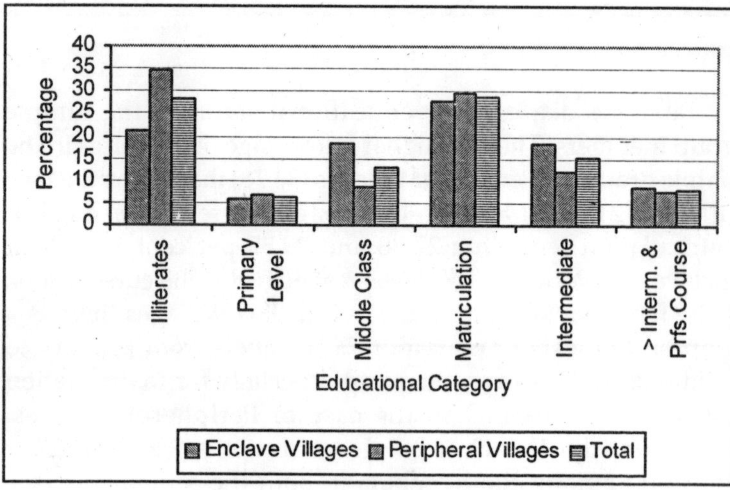

Fig. 4.3: Showing Educational Status of the Sample SHG Members

A study on SHGs in the districts of Coimbatore, Perambaur and Tiruchirapalli of Tamil Nadu in reference to the educational status of the SHG women members presents that 27 per cent are illiterate, 31 per cent are with primary and 36 per cent with secondary education.[2]

Family Type, Housing and Residential Ownership

In the present sample study, the group members belong to two types of family, such as nuclear and joint family.[3] Table 4.5

shows the pattern of family type among the sample group members. In both type of villages, there are more nuclear families. In the Enclave Villages, 76.92 per cent group members belong to nuclear families, while 23.08 per cent members are from joint families. In the Peripheral Villages, the pattern is not different. The figures are 75.65 and 24.35 per cent respectively for nuclear and joint families. There has been a positive shift of attitude towards nuclear way of living. This is primarily because of interest towards personal achievement to cope with the progressive world. The Enclave Villages are more towards nuclear families but the difference is quite negligible with that of Peripheral Villages. There is shrinking resource base and economic compulsion for the families in the Enclave Villages. There is feeling of insecurity among the members in the family. In addition, here the space is one of the scarce resources. Therefore, joint families are still at large in the Enclave Villages than the Peripheral Villages.

Table 4.5: Type of the Family among the Sample SHG Members

Type of Family	*Enclave Villages*		*Peripheral Villages*		*Total*	
	No.	*%*	*No.*	*%*	*No.*	*%*
Nuclear Family	80	76.92	87	75.65	167	76.26
Joint Family	24	27.08	28	24.35	52	23.74
Total	**104**	**100.00**	**115**	**100.00**	**219**	**100.00**

Source: Field Survey, 2008.

Table 4.6 shows the type of houses, where the group members live in. All the group members in the Peripheral Villages have *pacca* (cemented) houses. In the Enclave Villages, 98 per cent of group members have *pacca* houses leaving a few who dwells in the *kachha*[4] houses (only 2 per cent). The Enclave Villages include unauthorised colonies, which are basically occupied by the poor people, migrated to Delhi in search of livelihood. The Peripheral Villages are permanent in nature having proper settlements since many generations. The opportunities for the safe dwelling programme of the Government that flow to the villages at the periphery are yet to be enjoyed by the inhabitants at the unauthorised colonies. In addition, in the Peripheral Villages, the common property resource puts members in a better way than their counterparts in the Enclave Villages. The villages provide solid socio-economic platform with a scope for variety of resources through the inheritance of ancestral property. Enclave Villages are recent with limited scope and choice for resources.

Table 4.6: Type of House among the Sample SHG Members

Type of House	*Enclave Villages*		*Peripheral Villages*		*Total*	
	No.	*%*	*No.*	*%*	*No.*	*%*
Kachha House	2	1.92	—	—	2	0.91
Pacca House	102	98.08	115	100.00	217	99.09
Total	**104**	**100.00**	**115**	**100.00**	**219**	**100.00**

Source: Field Survey, 2008.

Table 4.7 displays the type of residences among the sample SHG members. This classification is based on the ownership, such as own residence and residence taken on rent. Most of the group members (90.38 per cent) have their own residences and 9.62 per cent of members stay on rented accommodation in the Enclave Villages. Whereas, 99.13 per cent of group members have own residences in the Peripheral Villages. The group members in these villages have at least their own houses, whether adequately furnished or not. Contrary to this, the Enclave Villages are urbanised, accommodating the people from outside on rent who come to earn livelihood. Here, the scope for institutional profit is high. There is exclusive economic differentiation and always demand for the house on rent, as these places are constantly touched by the floating or transient population.

My personal interaction with the SHG members in the Enclave Villages reiterates that at the time of SHG formation the members are chosen with one of the basic criteria having own residence. The rented persons are given least preference because they may change their residence anytime for the better opportunity elsewhere. Their constant mobility may harm the

SHG stability, which works as an enterprise with the aim of 'going concern'[5]. SHGs are small groups of up to 20 persons, who come together with the intention of saving and rotating credit among the members. Once these groups are stabilized, they are accorded formal support from the banking system so as to widen their lending capacities.

Table 4.7: Type of Residence among the Sample SHG Members

Residence Type	*Enclave Villages*		*Peripheral Villages*		*Total*	
	No.	*%*	*No.*	*%*	*No.*	*%*
Own	94	90.38	114	99.13	208	94.98
Rent	10	9.62	1	0.87	11	5.02
Total	**104**	**100.00**	**115**	**100.00**	**219**	**100.00**

Source: Field Survey, 2008.

Place of Birth and Migration

Table 4.8 shows the place of birth of SHG members. It distinguishes the members who were born in Delhi and those born outside Delhi. It is found that almost 49.04 per cent of sample SHG members were born in Delhi and rest of the members (50.96 per cent) are migrants to Delhi as far as the Enclave settlements are concerned. In the Peripheral Villages, almost 68.7 per cent of SHG members were born outside Delhi, while the rest of the members (31.3 per cent) were born in Delhi. The persons who were born outside Delhi had migrated to the city. There may be effect of neighbourhood as the Peripheral Villages are at the proximity with the adjoining areas of other states.

Table 4.8: Place of Birth among the Sample SHG Members

Place of Birth	*Enclave Villages*		*Peripheral Villages*		*Total*	
	No.	*%*	*No.*	*%*	*No.*	*%*
Delhi	51	49.04	36	31.30	87	39.73
Outside Delhi	53	50.96	79	68.70	132	60.27
Total	**104**	**100.00**	**115**	**100.00**	**219**	**100.00**

Source: Field Survey, 2008.

Table 4.9 describes the person who migrated to Delhi among the sample SHG members. In Enclave Villages, it is found that 86.79 per cent of members out of the total members were born outside Delhi and have migrated to the city along with their husbands. In this case, respective husbands came first to the city few years back and settled down in one of these unauthorised colonies and later on their wives joined them. In the Peripheral Villages, almost 96.20 per cent members out of the total members were born outside Delhi and had self-migration induced by marriage (see Fig. 4.4). Their husbands are the natives of the village and their migration is due to the social compulsion. In contrast, the migration is induced through push-pull factors for the SHG members in the Enclave

Table 4.9: Person Who Migrated to Delhi among the Sample SHG Members

Person Who Migrated	*Enclave Villages*		*Peripheral Villages*		*Total*	
	No.	*%*	*No.*	*%*	*No.*	*%*
Self	1	1.89	76	96.20	77	58.33
Husband	46	86.79	—	—	46	34.85
Parents	6	11.32	3	3.80	9	6.82
Total	**53**	**100.00**	**79**	**100.00**	**132**	**100.00**

Source: Field Survey, 2008.

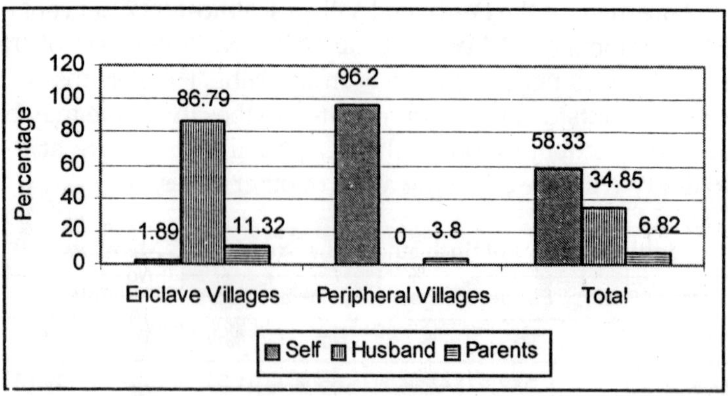

Fig. 4.4: Showing the Person Who Migrated to Delhi among the Sample SHG Members

Villages. This indicates that there is a lot of dependency among the members either on the parents or husbands.

Year of Joining SHGs

SHGs are established with the motive of empowering the downtrodden sections of the society who are left behind in the process of development initiated by various agencies/ departments. The target group primarily consists of the women, the children, the small and marginal farmers, the grass-root level entrepreneurs, the slum dwellers, the dejected and distressed. In the present sample study, all the members of SHGs happened to be women. Table 4.10 depicts the year of joining SHGs by the sample members. It is found that over the years there has been a rising trend among the members to join the SHGs. A little less than 5 per cent of sample members had joined the SHGs up to the year 2000. In the years 2001 and 2002, the membership slightly increased to 5.94 per cent. However, the catch was 15.98 per cent by 2003 and 2004, after which it travelled to 44.29 per cent by the end of 2008 (see Fig. 4.5). In Enclave Villages, the rise in the membership to the group was slow over the period up to 2004. It was then 24.04 per cent in between the years 2005 and 2006. In recent years (2007 and 2008), 56.73 per cent of sample members had joined the SHGs. However, the table depicts that only 5.22 per cent members had joined the group up to the year 2000 in the Peripheral Villages. By the next two years (2001 and 2002), only 6.09 per cent

Table 4.10: Year of Joining to the Group by the Sample SHG Members

Year of Joining	*Enclave Villages*		*Peripheral Villages*		*Total*	
	No.	*%*	*No.*	*%*	*No.*	*%*
2000 & Before	4	3.85	6	5.22	10	4.57
2001 & 2002	6	5.77	7	6.09	13	5.94
2003 & 2004	10	9.62	25	21.74	35	15.98
2005 & 2006	25	24.04	39	33.91	64	29.22
2007 & 2008	59	56.73	38	33.04	97	44.29
Total	**104**	**100.00**	**115**	**100.00**	**219**	**100.00**

Source: Field Survey, 2008.

members had joined the group. The significant rise was observed in the subsequent years. It was 21.74 per cent in 2003 and 2004, which rose to 33.91 per cent in 2005 and 2006. However, it came down to 33.04 per cent in 2007 and 2008.

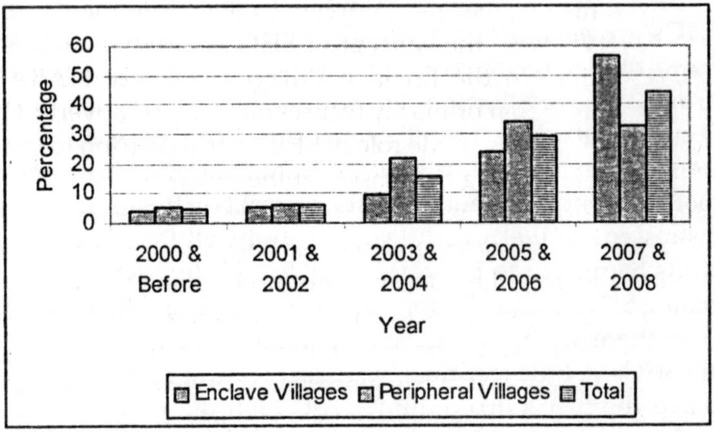

Fig. 4.5: Showing Year of Joining SHGs by Sample Members

The possible reasons for the rising trend of members joining the SHGs may relate to the following:

(i) The activity of the NGOs like MRYDO has been focused towards the microfinance aspect as the funding agencies primarily the NABARD, RMK, DCW and GRC put their attention on eradication of poverty at the grassroots level in Delhi.

(ii) The incentive is entirely based on performance of the NGO, and the fund releasing mechanism is a controlled phenomenon. In other words, the performance decides the level of incentive for the NGO from the funding agencies. Therefore, the NGO acts a facilitator.

(iii) It takes time to introduce new concepts in society. The society is primarily sensitive towards negative aspects rather than its benefits. There is always an 'acceptance timing', which focuses on its pros and cons. The other elements like the traditional money-lenders and economically well off sections in the society might have created a vacuum in the mind of poor as the group formation might dismantle their age old 'lavish and monopolistic' business attitude. This might have reduced the membership process in the initial years in the Enclave and Peripheral Villages. In the Peripheral Villages, the concept of SHG was better understood than in the Enclave Villages, because NABARD's initiation primarily focuses on the rural poverty. Urban poverty and the role of SHG is an extension to the idea of covering the masses at the grassroots.

(iv) Proper attention has been extended by the agencies and the NGO to enhance the capacity building process among the poor by concentrating on the formation of groups, thus expanding the base of SHGs. The increased group membership, in the recent years, indicates that SHG is a benefit driven concept. Thus, it is now welcomed by the majority.

(v) In addition, there is awareness factor, which works as an undercurrent. It is more conspicuous in the recent years. It is prominent in the Peripheral Villages followed by the Enclave Villages. The initiation of SHG concept has been basically focusing the rural areas and this is an extension of the SHG methodology to cover the urban poor.

One of the studies of NABARD depicts that when asked why they joined the SHG, 88 per cent of SHG members interviewed said that the primary reason for their joining was that it gave them the opportunity and motivation to save money regularly.[6]

Sources of Motivation

Table 4.11 shows the sources that motivate the people to join SHGs. There are internal and external sources. To some extent family exerts influence on its members to join SHGs. It is found that over 4 per cent people are influenced by the family tc join SHGs followed by 41.55 per cent through neighbours, friends and relatives, and 54.34 per cent by the NGOs. It is the employees/staff of NGOs who are in constant touch with the local people in order to motivate them to join the SHGs (see Fig. 4.6). By and large, the pattern remains same for both the settlements (i.e., Enclave and Peripheral Villages). In the Enclave Villages, 5.77 per cent of sample members are influenced by the family itself, which is higher than in Peripheral Villages (2.61 per cent). The neighbours, friends and relatives have greater impact on the sample members (43.48 per cent) of the Peripheral Villages than those in the Enclave Villages (39.42 per cent). However, the impact of NGOs more or less remains same for the Enclave Villages (54.81 per cent) and Peripheral Villages (53.91 per cent).

Table 4.11: Sources of Motivation by the Sample SHG Members

Sources of Motivation	*Enclave Villages*		*Peripheral Villages*		*Total*	
	No.	*%*	*No.*	*%*	*No.*	*%*
Family Members	6	5.77	3	2.61	9	4.11
Neighbour/Friends/ Relatives	41	39.42	50	43.48	91	41.55
NGO	57	54.81	62	53.91	119	54.34
Total	**104**	**100.00**	**115**	**100.00**	**219**	**100.00**

Source: Field Survey, 2008.

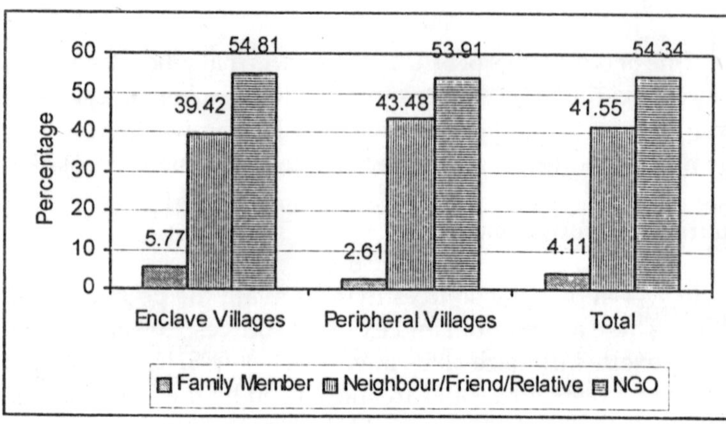

Fig. 4.6: Showing the Sources of Motivation by the Sample SHG Members

The possible reasons for this kind of pattern may be attributed to the following factors:

(i) The kind of commitment shown by the NGOs is to build up a considerable number of groups. It is either to match their target under the circumstances that operate in the purview of the funding agencies or as a part of the assimilation process in the society to strengthen the masses at the grassroots to address the problem.

(ii) Other than the external sources to influence, there are continuous sources of interaction through neighbours, friends and relatives, which work effectively giving motivational feedback to the people in the Peripheral Villages. These sources are wider and effective than the motivation drawn from the family in the kind of environment or social stratum where exposure is less among the members within the family in the Enclave Villages.

Size of Self-Help Groups

Table 4.12 presents the size of SHGs of the sample members. From the Table 4.12, it is found that 82.19 per cent sample members belong the SHGs whose size comprises of 20 members followed by 19 members (9.59 per cent) and 18 and less members (8.22 per cent) (see Fig. 4.7). As mentioned in the earlier chapters, the size of the group is not to exceed 20 members.In the Enclave Villages, 78.85 per cent sample members are from SHGs whose size comprises of 20 members followed by 19 members (11.54 per cent) and 18 and less members (9.62 per cent). In the Peripheral Villages, 85.22 per cent sample members belong to SHGs whose size comprises of 20 members followed by 19 members (7.83 per cent) and 18 and less members (6.96 per cent).

Table 4.12: Group Size of the Sample SHG Members

Group Size	*Enclave Villages*		*Peripheral Villages*		*Total*	
	No.	*%*	*No.*	*%*	*No.*	*%*
20 Members	82	78.85	98	85.22	180	82.19
19 Members	12	11.54	9	7.83	21	9.59
18 & Less Members	10	9.62	8	6.96	18	8.22
Total	**104**	**100.00**	**115**	**100.00**	**219**	**100.00**

Source: Field Survey, 2008.

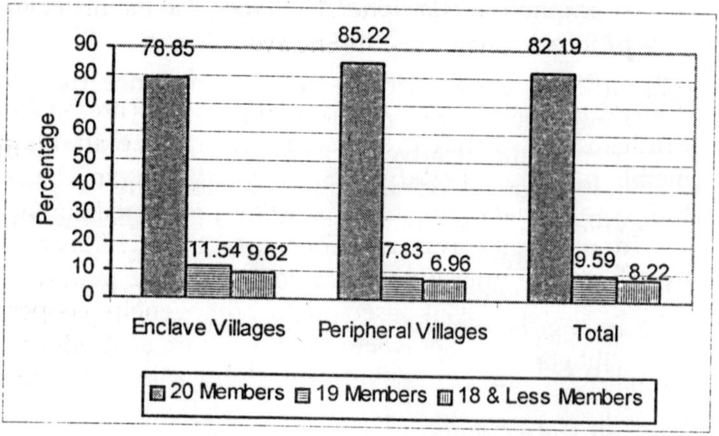

Fig. 4.7: Showing the Group Size of the Sample SHG Members

The possible reasons may be attributed to the factors given below:

(i) As a matter of policy of the NABARD, the NGOs have been instructed to keep size of the group with a maximum limit of 20 members. Therefore, a considerable number of SHGs had 20 members. Exceeding the size of the group beyond 20 members would attract its registration under the Society Registration Act of India.

(ii) No human groups are permanent in nature. The members of a group do join and retire. There has been effort by the SHGs to keep the strength of members optimum so that higher the numbers, higher is the savings and it facilitates better in terms of annual returns and sanction of loan from the banks.

(iii) The Enclave Villages show that the SHGs have a higher attrition as a part of members do migrate out of the area because of change in the place of work of husbands, change of temporary accommodations which have been taken on rent, or due to several factors like unmarried members go out of the area after marriage, etc. Therefore, it is really a difficult task to keep the size of the SHGs intact. In the Peripheral Villages, the members are less volatile than those in Enclave Villages.

A study conducted on SHGs in the Tirupati area of Andhra Pradesh shows that the average group size stands at 12 members.[7] Another study on SHGs functioning in 11 states of India shows that the average size of the groups is 16 members.[8]

To sum up, it may be mentioned here that SHG is a medium by which the microfinance is routed to the people at the grassroots. The SHG is based on the homogeneity, cooperation and collectivism. The socio-demographic and educational status of members plays an important role in the field of microfinance. Almost 85 per cent of group members are in the age of 21 to 50 years in the Enclave Villages, which is a bit lower than in the Peripheral Villages (87 per cent). The average age of sample members is 37.8 years, which is 35.9 years and 39.5 years in the Enclave and Peripheral Villages respectively. The average number of children per member woman, is 2.73. The average household size is 4.9 individuals. There is no much difference observed between the settlements. In the present sample study, married women members constitute 90 per cent. There are widows who are also members of SHGs. However, there are unmarried members found in the Enclave settlements. A larger concentration of members has qualification of matriculation. The spread of illiteracy is larger at the Peripheral Villages (34.78 per cent) than the Enclave Villages (21.15 per cent). Out of the sample of Enclave Villages, 76.92 per cent have nuclear family, 98.08 per cent sample members have *pacca* houses and 90.38 per cent members have own house. Out of the sample of Peripheral Villages, 75.65 per cent have nuclear family, all sample members have *pacca* houses and 99 per cent members have own house. While, 68.7 per cent of members were born outside Delhi in case of members of the Peripheral Villages, the corresponding figure for Enclave Villages is 51 per cent. Marriage induced migration is observed in the Peripheral Villages (96 per cent). Whereas, in Enclave Villages, 98 per cent members had come to Delhi along with their parents or husbands. From the joining pattern of the members, it is observed that the concept of SHG is more popular in recent years when 44.29 per cent have joined the group in the years 2007 and 2008. The motivation to join the group is an open phenomenon, yet NGOs play a great role (54.34 per cent) followed by the neighbours, friends and relatives (41.55 per cent). Family has least role in the motivational process. The group size matters for the prosperity of the group. It is observed that 82.19 per cent members belong to the group where the groups have 20 members. Thus, the comparative sketch between the settlements on account of socio-demographic and educational status of SHG members provides knowledge that there are two distinct patterns of life which not only influences the self as an individual, but the family members and the groups as well.

NOTES AND REFERENCES

1. C. Dash (2006): *Social Ecology and Demographic Structure: Narratives and Discourses*. New Delhi: Concept Publishing Company, p. 120.
2. M. Manimekalai and G. Rajeswari (2001): Nature and Performance of Informal Self-Helf Groups—A Case from Tamil Nadu. *Indian Journal of Agricultural Economics*, Vol. 56, No. 3, p. 453.
3. 'Nuclear family' is a type of family, where the husband, wife and their children live under one roof. Until the children are unmarried, they live with their parents. 'Joint family' is a type of family, where the married couples live with their parents and children. The traditional Indian society had bright scope for the joint family. Due to the growth of urbanization and industrialization, the joint family segregates into economically potential nuclear families.
4. The house is not cemented one. It includes temporary roof with

polythene or plastic sheet and the walls are made out of firewood and bamboo.

5. 'Going concern' refers to an enterprise, which is established with a philosophy of working for an indefinite period.
6. *'Impact of Self-Help Groups (Group Processes) on the Social/Empowerment Status of Women Members in Southern India'*, commissioned jointly by MYRADA and NABARD, designed by MYRADA and conducted by A.C. Neilson ORG-MARG (SRC), published by NABARD in November 2002 and released at the Seminar on SHG-Bank Linkage organised by NABARD at New Delhi on 25th and 26th November 2002 to commemorate 10 years of SHG-Bank Linkage, Table 3.9, p.22 found at http://*planning.kar.nic.in/khdr2005/English/Main%20Report/ 14-chapter.pdf*
7. S.K. Datta and M. Raman (2001): Can Heterogeneity and Social Cohesion Coexist in Self-Help Groups?: An Evidence from Group Lending in Andhra Pradesh. *Indian Journal of Agricultural Economics,* Vol. 56, No. 3, p. 389.
8. V. Puhazhendhi and K.J.S. Satyasai (2001): Economic and Social Empowerment of Rural Poor through Self-Help Groups, *Indian Journal of Agricultural Economics,* Vol. 56, No. 3, p. 450.

5

Economic Profile of Members and Spatial Linkage of the Sample Villages

Household occupation is an indicator of the income. Income is like fuel of a vehicle. Without its use, no household can run smoothly. Its absence or presence makes things different. In a third world country like India, the crux lies in the level of income. There is clear-cut dichotomy in having it or not. The present chapter prioritises the sketch on the source of income and different types of occupation of the SHG members. It also tries to put light on average annual income and expenditure of households of the SHG members. The emphasis has been made to understand the role of spatial linkages of the sample Enclave and Peripheral Villages with the important destinations.

Occupation of SHG Members

Table 5.1 presents the occupational structure of the sample SHG members belonging to the Enclave and Peripheral Villages. In Enclave Villages, it is found that a larger number of SHG members spend their time as homemaker (65.38 per cent). Second to this category, 13.46 per cent members are engaged in services. There are students (4.81 per cent), unskilled and skilled labourers (6.73 per cent) and professional workers, shopkeepers and dairy businesswomen (9.62 per cent). The picture on occupation in the Peripheral Villages is slightly different. In the sample, 59.13 per cent of SHG members spend their time in homemaking followed by the members (33.91 per cent) in professional work, shop keeping and dairy business. There are no members as student. Only 2.61 per cent members are unskilled and skilled labourers. However, some members (4.35 per cent) resort to both private and government services. As such in the sample study, it is found that a large section of the SHG members are homemakers (62.10 per cent) followed by those involved in professional work, shop keeping and dairy business (22.37 per cent), service (8.68 per cent), unskilled and skilled labour (4.57 per cent) and students (2.28 per cent) (see Fig. 5.1).

Table 5.1: Occupational Structure of the Sample SHG Members

Occupational Structure	*Enclave Villages*		*Peripheral Villages*		*Total*	
	No.	*%*	*No.*	*%*	*No.*	*%*
Homemaker	68	65.38	68	59.13	136	62.10
Unskilled & Skilled Labour	7	6.73	3	2.61	10	4.57
Professional Work, Shop Keeping & Dairy Business	10	9.62	39	33.91	49	22.37
Service (Pvt. & Govt.)	14	13.46	5	4.35	19	8.68
Student	5	4.81	—	—	5	2.28
Total	**104**	**100.00**	**115**	**100.00**	**219**	**100.00**

Source: Field Survey, 2008.

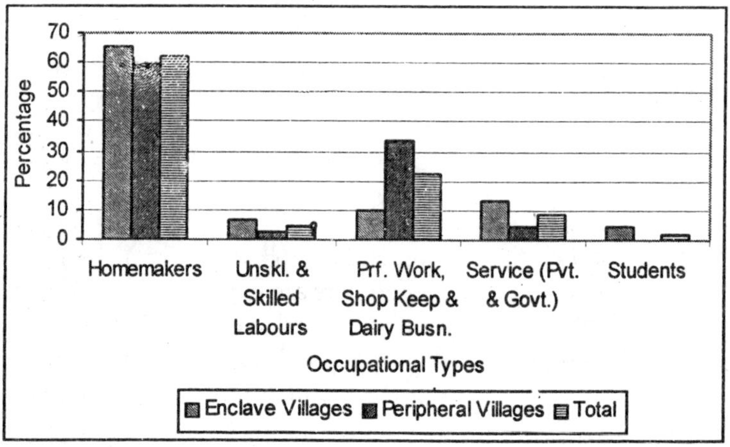

Fig. 5.1: Occupational Structure of the Sample SHG Members

The difference in occupation in both the settlements may be due to the following factors:

(i) Enclave Villages provide occupation, which is suited to urban life style. The scope is expanded towards services in both private and government organisations. The educational status of members also determines the present occupation. Even younger population like students resort to be member of the SHGs.
(ii) In the Peripheral Villages, other than homemakers, some members carryout dairy business. The village lifestyle provides scope for the domestication of cow and buffalo. However, the outdoor occupations are less preferred in this kind of settlement.
(iii) Economic specialisation is based on the economic rationalisation. In the Enclave Villages, there is a unique urban mode of occupational structure i.e., adherence to either home-making or services. In contrast to this, the members in the Peripheral Villages are primarily occupied by a variety of occupations such as profession-based work, shop-keeping and dairy business other than home-making.

Annual Household Income of SHG Members

Table 5.2 highlights the income structure of households of the SHG members. In the income category of below Rs. 30,000, there are almost equal percentage of members in the Enclave Villages (6.73 per cent) and Peripheral Villages (6.09 per cent). A major chunk of members (44.29 per cent) belongs to the income category of Rs. 30,001-Rs. 60,000, which is 51.92 per cent and 37.39 per cent in the Enclave and Peripheral Villages respectively. In the Enclave Villages, 25 per cent members belong to the higher income category (above Rs. 90,000), and 16.35 per cent members are in the middle level (i.e., Rs. 60,001-90,000). However, almost equal percentage of members (i.e., 28.70 per cent and 27.82 per cent) belongs to the income category of Rs. 60,001-Rs. 90,000 and above Rs. 90,000 respectively in the Peripheral Villages. In total, 22.83 and 26.49 per cent of SHG members have an annual household income of Rs. 60,001-Rs. 90,000 and above Rs. 90,000 respectively (see Fig. 5.2).

Table 5.2: Annual Income Structure of the Sample SHG Members

Annual Income Category (in Rs.)	*Enclave Villages*		*Peripheral Villages*		*Total*	
	No.	*%*	*No.*	*%*	*No.*	*%*
< 30,001	7	6.73	7	6.09	14	6.39
30,001-60,000	54	51.92	43	37.39	97	44.29
60,001-90,000	17	16.35	33	28.70	50	22.83
> 90,000	26	25.00	32	27.82	58	26.49
Total	**104**	**100.00**	**115**	**100.00**	**219**	**100.00**

Source: Field Survey, 2008.

The difference in the household income may be attributed to the following reasons:

(i) In the Enclave settlement there is polarisation in the income level. Larger sections of members belong to lower income category. The need arises out of compulsion for the survival, as the urban mode of life demands for employment, which is readily available for them.

(ii) In the Peripheral settlement there is uniformity in the level of household income. Members have substitute income from agriculture, dairy, other businesses, etc. making the income level higher than the Enclave settlements.

(iii) In the Peripheral Villages, the resource distribution is based on the criteria of inheritance. There is accumulation of property over the generations. In the Enclave Villages, the accumulation of property is a recent phenomenon, which means the accumulation process may be from the current or from father's generation. One has to do a lot of struggle to survive rather than thinking of accumulation. This can be viewed from the income category of members, majority of whom fall in the second category of lower-middle income category.

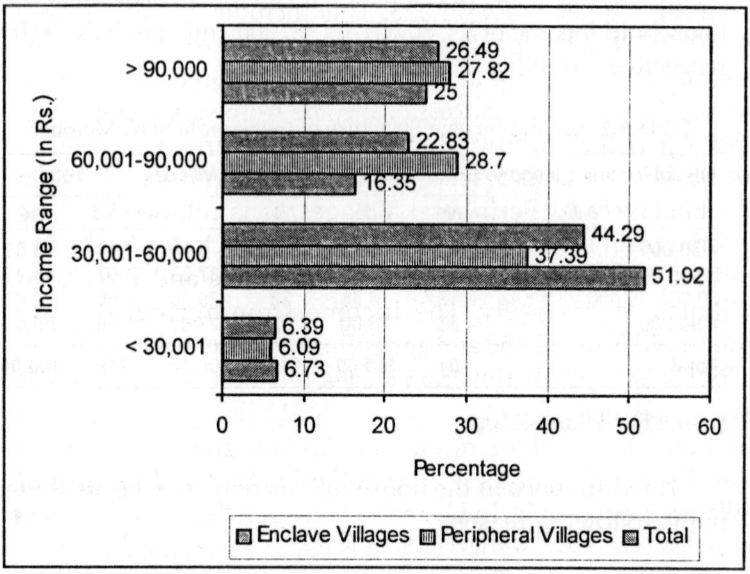

Fig. 5.2: Annual Income Structure of the Sample SHG Members

Income and Expenditure Pattern

Despite the widespread use of income as a measure of household welfare, there is much to recommend the use of consumption. Indeed, standard economic arguments suggest that consumption expenditure will better reflect expected lifetime resources and many economists have been unequivocal in advocating its use.[1] Slesnick, for example, suggests that "from a theoretical perspective it is more appropriate to evaluate poverty using a consumption based measure of household welfare".[2] Traditionally, economists and policy analysts have tended to view the household as a unit that pools income and allocates resources for consumption, production, and investment.[3] As far as the poor are concerned, savings are made, not out of a surplus of income, but by cutting down some expenditure somewhere. In theory income minus expenditure is savings; in the case of the poor, the reality is income minus savings is expenditure.[4]

Table 5.3 shows the average annual income of SHG members with household occupation. It is understood that the average annual income (AAI) per SHG member household from all sources is Rs. 71,326. This includes Rs. 68,054 and Rs. 74,285 for the Enclave Villages and Peripheral Villages respectively. Looking at the sources of income, households having two or more sources of income from service, business and agriculture show highest average annual income of Rs. 95,445, which is respectively Rs. 77,600 and Rs. 97,357 in the Enclave and Peripheral Villages. It is followed by the income from service of Rs. 78,398, which includes Rs. 76,012 and Rs. 81,977 per household in the Enclave and Peripheral Villages respectively. The income from agriculture per household is Rs. 41,150 and agriculture and business combined is Rs. 63,000 in the Peripheral Villages, but there is no household having income from these sources in the Enclave Villages. There are pensioners, whose income per annum goes to Rs. 51,909 with Rs. 57,167 and Rs. 45,600 in the Enclave and Peripheral Villages respectively. In business, there is no much difference between these two settlements. It is Rs. 63,759, which includes Rs. 64,071 and Rs. 63,467 per annum per household in the Enclave and Peripheral Villages respectively (see Fig. 5.3).

Table 5.3: Average Annual Income (AAI) (in Rs.) of Households of the Sample SHG Members

Household Occupation	*Enclave Villages*	*Peripheral Villages*	*Total*
Labourer (Skilled & Unskilled)	39,200	35,844	37,942
Agriculture	—	41,150	41,150
Business	64,071	63,467	63,759
Service (Govt. & Pvt.)	76,012	81,977	78,398
Pensioner	57,167	45,600	51,909
Agriculture & Business	—	63,000	63,000
Service/Pensioner & Business/ Agriculture	77,600	97,357	95,445
Total	**68,054**	**74,285**	**71,326**

Source: Field Survey, 2008.

Table 5.4 presents the average annual expenditure (AAE) per household of the SHG members. It is understood that the average annual expenditure (AAE) of the sample households in this study stands at Rs. 60,798. This includes Rs. 56,213 and Rs. 64,864 per household in the Enclave and Peripheral Villages respectively. The cursory look at different heads of expenditure

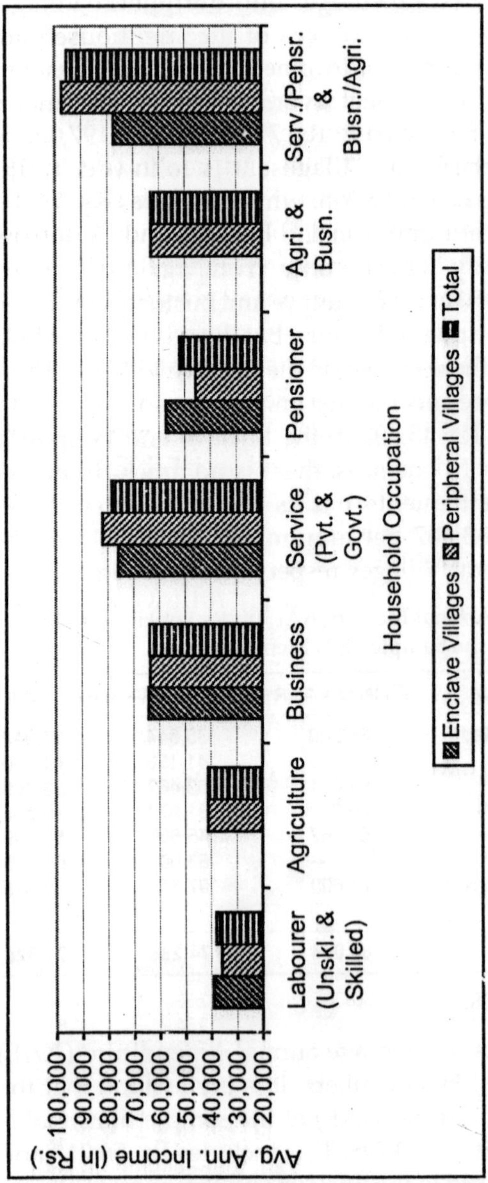

Fig. 5.3: Average Annual Income of the Households of Sample SHG Members

reflects that a major chunk of expenditure is occurred on livelihood consumption (Rs. 31,747) followed by education (Rs. 14,481). Other striking heads of expenditure are like loan repayment (Rs. 12,688), house rent (Rs. 11,891), husband's requirement (Rs. 6,873) and conveyance (Rs. 4,477). The expenditure on clothing (Rs. 1,734) and health (Rs. 1,219) remains low in comparison to consumer durables (Rs. 2,466). The expenditure on gift and social obligation finds a narrow space in the annual sheet of expenditure, *i.e.* just Rs. 834. In the Enclave Villages, a major chunk of money goes for livelihood consumption (Rs. 30,072) followed by education (Rs. 12,627) and house rent (Rs. 12,360). Loan repayment also takes away some share of income (Rs. 9,484) followed by husband's requirement (Rs. 6,463). The expenditure on conveyance stands at Rs. 3,791. The expenditure on gift and social obligation (Rs. 741), health (Rs. 1,097), clothing (Rs. 1,612) remains low in comparison to consumer durables (Rs. 2,250). Similarly, in the Peripheral settlement, a major share of income goes for livelihood consumption (Rs. 33,203) followed by loan repayment (Rs. 16,253) and education of children (Rs. 16,161). Husband's requirement (Rs. 7,251), house rent (Rs. 7,200) and expenditure on conveyance (Rs. 5,365) have some impact on the annual income of households. Like Enclave settlement,

Table 5.4: Average Annual Expenditure (AAE) (in Rs.) of Households of the Sample SHG Members

Head of Expenditure	*Enclave Villages*	*Peripheral Villages*	*Total*
Education	12,627	16,161	14,481
Health	1,097	1,325	1,219
Loan Repayment	9,484	16,253	12,688
Livelihood	30,072	33,203	31,747
Husband's Requirement	6,463	7,251	6,873
Clothing	1,612	1,838	1,734
House Rent	12,360	7,200	11,891
Utensils	236	417	348
Consumer Durables	2,250	2,579	2,466
Gift and Social Obligations	741	907	834
Conveyance	3,791	5,365	4,477
Total	56,213	64,864	60,798

Source: Field Survey, 2008.

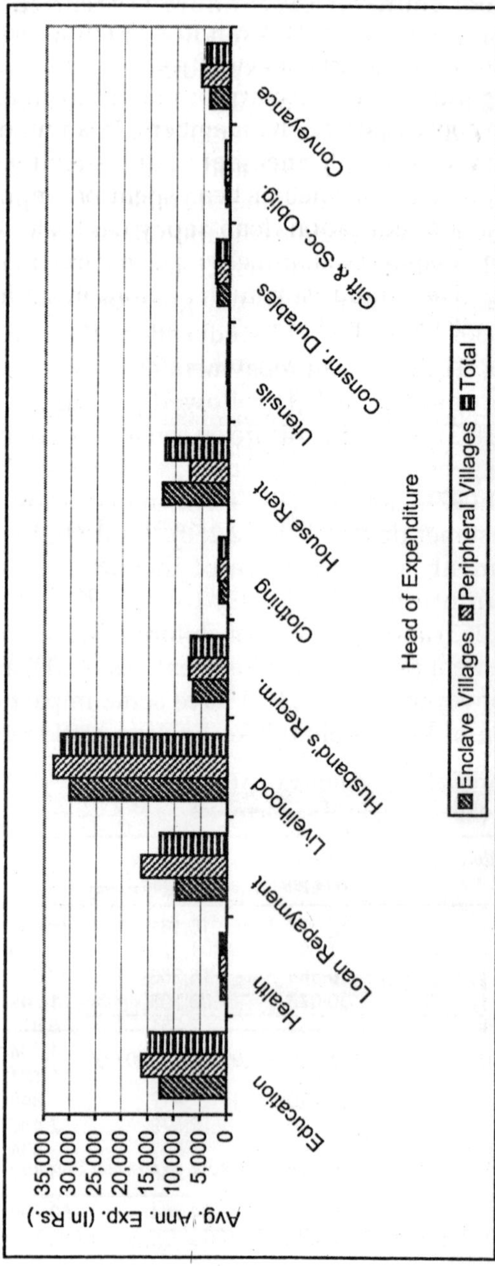

Fig. 5.4: Average Annual Expenditure of Households of the Sample SHG Members

the expenditure on gift and social obligation (Rs. 907), health (Rs. 1,325), clothing (Rs. 1,838) remains low in comparison to consumer durables (Rs. 2,579) (see Fig. 5.4).

Table 5.5 highlights the summary of annual income and expenditure per household of SHG members. It is found that the household of the sample members have surplus even though a major share of income has been spent on important heads like livelihood, education, loan repayment, etc. From Fig. 5.5, it has been observed that higher the income higher is the expenditure. The annual surplus per household in the sample is Rs. 10,528 which includes Rs. 11,841 and Rs. 9,421 in the Enclave and Peripheral Villages respectively.

Table 5.5: Surplus (in Rs.) per Annum of the Households of the Sample SHG Members

Parameters	*Enclave Villages*	*Peripheral Villages*	*Total*
Avg. Annual Income	68,054	74,285	71,326
Avg. Annual Expenditure	56,213	64,864	60,798
Annual Surplus	11,841	9,421	10,528

Source: Field Survey, 2008.

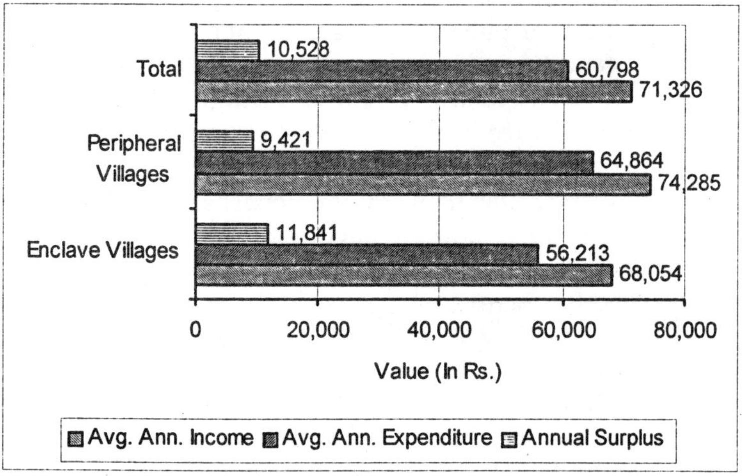

Fig. 5.5: Annual Surplus of the Households of the Sample SHG Members

The explanation for the above pattern may be attributed to the following factors:

(i) In this sample study, it is found that the expenditure depends on the level of income. For any human society, income is an opportunity and consumption is the preparedness for availing the opportunity, because income is realised through consumption pattern. Other factors like capacity to earn affect pattern as well. Therefore, there is a direct relationship between income and expenditure.

(ii) The attitude towards savings is learnt overtime. It is possible when we are able to satisfy the minimum needs of consumption. It is also a cultural perception towards household budget. Higher level of surplus in the enclave settlements may be attributed to the lowering of expenditure through economic rationalisation. Economic rationalisation is an outcome of an urban outlook, and insecurity towards future dominates the mind of Enclave Villagers. Higher level of expenditure is indicative of showing social status in the villages of the Peripheral settlements. In other words, income and expenditure follow a status symbol in the Peripheral Villages. Higher income leads to expenditure, thus minimising the annual surplus. In reference to the Enclave Villages, income and expenditure pattern follow a rational approach. Expenditure is controlled and based on the justification to spend rather than any emotional backup. The feeling of insecurity is very much with the members in the Enclave settlement; therefore, saving for the future is a need for them.

(iii) The distance of the villages with the important destinations, to some extent, casts a role in the expenditure pattern. For example, the expenditure on conveyance and expenditure on education as to commute between the schools and the residence, etc. is important. This factor has been noticed from the data analysis.

According to Delhi Government's estimates of State Domestic Product (SDP) 2004-05, the per capita income of Delhi at current prices has increased from Rs 49,494 in 2003-04 to Rs 53,976. Delhi's per capita income has left the national average way behind. The national per capita income at current prices is Rs 23,241 which makes Delhi's more than twice as much.[5] Twenty top boom cities in India are projected to have their household income grow at 10 per cent annually over the next eight years, and they already account for 60 per cent of the surplus income (income minus expenditure) generated at present. These 20 cities are divided in three groups: 'Megacities' (eight largest cities in terms of population and overall consumer markets) like Mumbai and Delhi; 'Boomtowns' (next set of seven big population cities with high expenditure per household) like Surat and Coimbatore; and 'Niche Cities' (five cities with relatively smaller population but above national-average household spend) like Faridabad and Jalandhar. These cities account for just a tenth of the country's population, but generate around 60 per cent of India's surplus income and around a third (31 per cent) of disposable income. These 20 cities have been accounted for just under $100-billion of consumption expenditure in 2007-08.[6]

Spatial Linkage of Sample Villages

The spatial linkages play an important role in the development of a place. The link with the important destinations not only keeps the people to solve the needs of life but also acculturates them with the flow of information and exposure. The villages that are nearer to the destinations have better advantage than the farther villages. This may be understood in relation to the time and space. The villages nearer to the important destinations may take little time to reach and the pressure of distance to cover them is also less in comparison to the far off villages. The nearer villages may attract the attention of developmental agencies as they can build pressure on them by their frequent visits. The physical science also justifies this, as the law of conduction of heat[7] advocates that the substance nearer to the heated element is hotter than the farther substances. Many anthropological studies point out that the greater traditions influence the little traditions surrounding them. "There is a constant interaction between the two levels of traditions."[8] The cultural epicentre has impact on the peripheries as it works like a condensed and capsulated element with multifaceted, vibrant and advanced economy, science and technology. The theory of diffusion reiterates that the flow of substance is from the higher concentration area to the lower ones. Hence, the study of spatial linkages has wider application in the context of 'Urban' 'Microfinance'.

In the present study, the villages/colonies in both categories of settlements have been seen through distance by road from important destinations. Altogether 22 villages with important destinations and the respective distance have been presented in Appendix 2. There are seven important destinations chosen such as district headquarter, C.D. Block (Community Development Block)/ward, police station, nearest town, nearest bus stop, nearest *mandi*[9] and local hat.[10] These destinations are vital links for the villages. The activities of the people in the Enclave and Peripheral Villages depend much on these destinations. In order to understand the role of these destinations, the distance indices have been calculated for each sample village in the Enclave and Peripheral areas of Delhi (see Chapter 3).

Table 5.6 presents the distance indices of the Enclave Villages. In the Enclave Villages, the distance indices vary in between 0.28 and 1.67. The villages in the high index (1.67 – 1.52) are Kapas Hera, Bijwasan and Laxman Puri. The villages in the medium index (1.52 – 0.91) are Surakh Pur Road and Nangli Sakrawati. The villages in the low index (0.91 – 0.62) are Shiv Enclave, Roshan Garden and Roshan Pura. The villages in the very low index (0.62 – 0.28) are Dharampura and Raghubir Block. The mean standard deviation is 0.50 with coefficient of variation 50 per cent.

Table 5.7 presents the distance indices of the Peripheral Villages. In the Peripheral Villages, the distance indices vary between 0.63 and 1.42. The villages in the high index (1.42 – 1.26)

Table 5.6: The Distance Indices of the Enclave Villages in the Study Area

Sl. No.	*Enclave Village*	*Distance Index*
1.	Raghubir Block (Prem Nagar)	0.28
2.	Roshan Garden	0.73
3.	Dharam Pura	0.44
4.	Surakh Pur Road	1.33
5.	Roshan Pura	0.62
6.	Shiv Enclave	0.78
7.	Bijwasan	1.58
8.	Nangli Sakrawati	1.03
9.	Kapas Hera	1.67
10.	Laxman Puri	1.52
Mean ($\bar{X}$)		1.00
Standard Deviation		0.50
Coefficient of Variation		50%

Where, the Ranges of Distance Indices are: High Index = 1.67 – 1.52, Medium Index = 1.52 – 0.91, Low Index = 0.91 – 0.62, and Very Low Index = 0.62 – 0.28.

Source: Field Survey, 2008.

are Baqar Garh, Hasan Pur and Qazi Pur. The villages in the medium index (1.26 – 0.99) are Dichaun, Khera Dabar and Pindwala Khurd. The villages in the low index (0.99 – 0.74) are Mahabir Vihar, Kair and Rewla Kham Pur. The villages in the very low index (0.74 – 0.63) are Surakh Pur, Surera and Jharoda. The mean standard deviation is 0.26 with coefficient of variation 26 per cent.

Table 5.8 presents distance indices and position of villages in the Enclave and Peripheral taken together. In the Peripheral Villages, the distance indices vary between 0.23 and 1.65. The villages in the high index (1.65 – 1.18) are Baqar Garh, Qazi Pur, Hasan Pur, Khera Dabar, Kapas Hera and Dichaun. The villages in the medium index (1.18 – 1.06) are Pindwala Khurd, Surakh Pur Road, Bijwasan, Laxman Puri and Mahabir Vihar. The villages in the low index (1.06 – 0.79) are Kair, Surera, Surakh Pur, Rewla Kham Pur, Nangli Sakrawati and Jharoda. The villages in the very low index (0.79 – 0.23) are Roshan Garden, Shiv Enclave, Roshan Pura, Dharam Pura and

Raghubir Block. The mean standard deviation is 0.39 with coefficient of variation 39 per cent.

Table 5.7: The Distance Indices of the Peripheral Villages in the Study Area

Sl. No.	*Peripheral Village*	*Distance Index*
1.	Mahabir Vihar	0.98
2.	Dichaun	1.20
3.	Surakh Pur	0.71
4.	Jharoda	0.63
5.	Surera	0.71
6.	Pindwala	0.99
7.	Hasan Pur	1.33
8.	Rewla Kham Pur	0.76
9.	Kair	0.84
10.	Baqar Garh	1.42
11.	Qazi Pur	1.31
12.	Khera Dabar	1.11
Mean ($\bar{X}$)		1.00
Standard Deviation		0.26
Coefficient of Variation		26%

Where, the Ranges of Distance Indices are: High Index = 1.42 – 1.26, Medium Index = 1.26 – 0.99, Low Index = 0.99 – 0.74, and Very Low Index = 0.74 – 0.63.

Source: Field Survey, 2008.

Figure. 5.6 shows the villages and their position in respect to the range of distance indices from high index to the very low index. It is observed that the villages nearer to the destinations show lower index than the farther villages. The villages with very low index are in complete advantageous position. The villages with low index are comparatively less advantageous than the villages in the category of very low index. Likewise, the villages in the medium index category are less advantageous than the low index category villages. The villages in the high index category are least advantageous than the other villages. The relationship between index value and advantageousness is indirectly proportional. That means, higher the index lower is the advantageousness. The advantageousness can be presented from lower order to higher order, i.e., high index<medium index<low index<very low index. Here the villages in the very low index category are the most advantaged ones.

Table 5.8: The Distance Indices and the Position of Villages in the Study Area

Sl. No.	*Village/Colony*	*Distance Index*
1.	Raghubir Block (Prem Nagar)	0.23
2.	Roshan Garden	0.63
3.	Dharam Pura	0.37
4.	Surakh Pur Road	1.16
5.	Roshan Pura	0.50
6.	Shiv Enclave	0.57
7.	Bijwasan	1.11
8.	Nangli Sakrawati	0.84
9.	Kapas Hera	1.31
10.	Laxman Puri	1.10
11.	Mahabir Vihar	1.08
12.	Dichaun	1.18
13.	Surakh Pur	0.89
14.	Jharoda	0.79
15.	Surera	0.89
16.	Pindwala Khurd	1.16
17.	Hasan Pur	1.58
18.	Rewla Kham Pur	0.86
19.	Kair	1.05
20.	Baqar Garh	1.65
21.	Qazi Pur	1.64
22.	Khera Dabar	1.38
Mean ($\bar{X}$)		1.00
Standard Deviation		0.39
Coefficient of Variation		39%

Where, the Ranges of Distance Indices are: High Index = 1.65 – 1.18, Medium Index = 1.18 – 1.06, Low Index = 1.06 – 0.79, and Very Low Index = 0.79 – 0.23.

Source: Field Survey, 2008.

In the context of Delhi it may be argued that over 62 per cent of its landmass falls under the urban areas. The villages, which are earlier in the rural Delhi, have been engulfed by urban areas. The decadal population growth between 1991 and 2001 for the rural areas has shown negative growth rate (-0.45

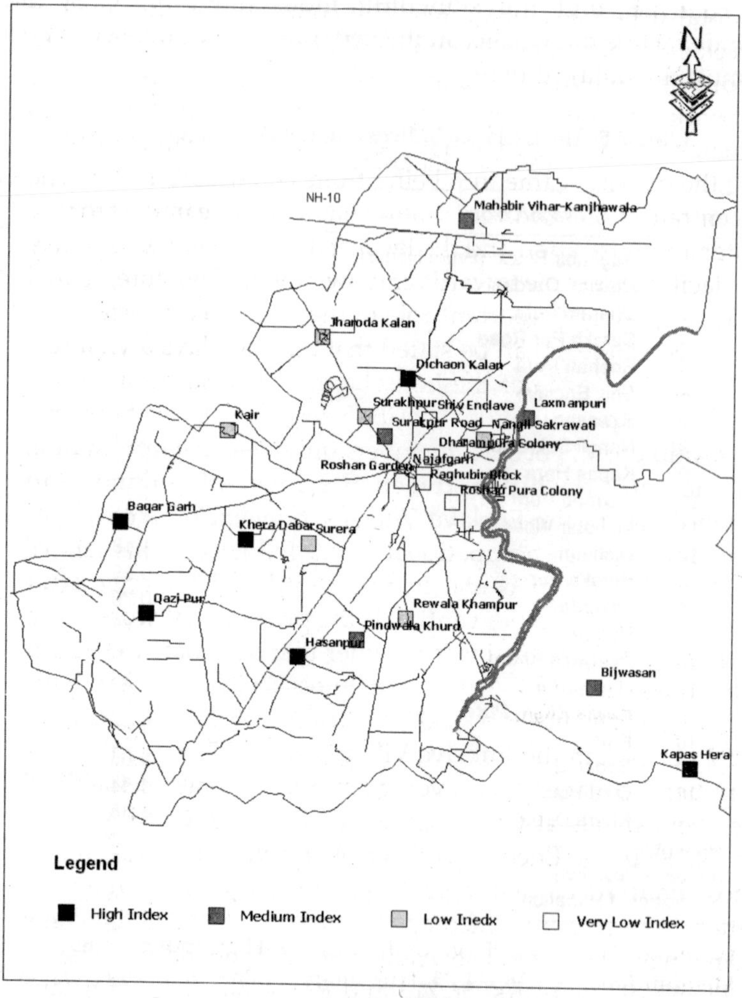

Fig. 5.6: Distance Indices of the Villages/Colonies in Najafgarh Area, Delhi, Year 2008-09

per cent) in comparison to 52.34 per cent in the urban areas (see Table 3.1, Chapter 3). There were 300 villages in Delhi in the year 1961; however, by the end of 2001, there were only 165 villages (Census, 2001). The declining trend of the number of villages implies that the areas of Delhi are surely going to be total urban agglomerates. The connectivity and level of development is rising. The physical distance is reduced by the improvised cellular communications. The administrative network has also been rising. For example, till 1996, Delhi remained a uni-district and it was bifurcated into nine districts and the districts came into being from 1st January 1997.[11] The decentralisation in administration has a positive impact for the better administration and the level of development. Ultimately this facilitates people towards empowerment. Therefore, spatial linkages play an important role in the microcredit sector.

To conclude, it can be stated that income plays a vital role in the maintenance of the household. The social profiles like education and occupational position decide the level of earning. The sample study of SHG members provides vital information on the relationship between the level of income and expenditure. In the Enclave Villages, homemakers (65.38 per cent) dominate the occupational profile followed by the service holders (13.46 per cent). In the Peripheral Villages after homemakers (59.13 per cent), it is the professional work, shop keeping and dairy business together that dominate (33.91 per cent) the occupational profile. Almost 44.29 members have annual income between Rs. 30,000 and Rs. 60,000 that includes 51.92 per cent in the Enclave Villages and 28.7 per cent in the Peripheral Villages. The average annual income of the SHG members stands at Rs. 71,326 which includes Rs. 68,054 and Rs. 74,285 in the Enclave and Peripheral Villages respectively. Those households with more than one source of income have better average annual income compared to those with income from singular source. The average annual expenditure stands at Rs. 60,798, with Rs. 56,213 and Rs. 64,864 in the Enclave Villages and Peripheral Villages respectively. In addition to the income and expenditure, the level of annual surplus of SHG members stands at Rs. 10,528. The annual surplus of members in the Enclave Villages is Rs. 11,841 and it is Rs. 9,421 in the Peripheral Villages. The reason of difference between the settlements may be due to the economic rationalisation in the Enclave Villages and the priority given to social status by the members in the Peripheral Villages. The distance of the villages from important destinations, to some extent, casts a role in the expenditure pattern. The villages that are near to the destinations like District HQ, C.D. Block HQ, police station, nearest town, *mandi*, local *hat*, etc. have better advantage than the farther villages. The coefficient of variation of distance index is 26 per cent and 39 per cent in the Enclave and Peripheral Villages respectively.

NOTES

1. R. Blundell and I. Preston (1996): 'Income, Expenditure and the Living Standards of UK Households', *Fiscal Studies*, Vol. 16, No. 3, pp. 40-54.
2. D.T. Slesnick (1993): 'Gaining Ground: Poverty in the Post-war United States', *Journal of Political Economy*, Vol. 101, p. 1 found at *http://www.jstor.org/pss/2138672*
3. *http://www. krpcds.org/report/minipercent20sukumar.pdf*
4. *http://www.planning.kar.nic.in/khdr2005/English/Mainper cent20Report/14-chapter (Box 14.4).pdf*
5. *The Times of India*, 22nd July, 2006 found at *http://timesofindia.indiatimes.com/articleshow/1789927.cms*
6. *The Economic Times*, 8th Aug.,2008 found at *http://www.ncaer.org/downloads/MediaClips/Press/Ecotimes-top20citieshold.pdf*
7. The matter that is nearer to the heated elements is hotter than the matter that is far by distance.
8. Y. Singh (1986): *Modernisation of Indian Traditions: A Systemic Study of Social Change*, Jaipur: Rawat Publications, p.13.
9. *Mandi* is a government administered trading centre.
10. *Hat* is a local daily, weekly or monthly regular market place.
11. Census of India (2001): *District Census Handbook*, Series-8, Delhi, Vol. 1, p. 29.

6

Impact Assessment of Microfinance Through Credit and Asset Structure

The basic concept of development banking and social banking implies that credit is used as a lever of development. Credit is an indispensable input for the development process, and an essential ingredient for effecting changes in the scale of production and technology. A large proportion of marginal and small farmers earns low income without savings of their own. They often depend on the sources of formal and informal credit. Strengthening formal credit source for provision of timely and adequate credit could help in poverty eradication.[1] Perpetual poverty and lack of adequate credit have remained the major constraints in economic upliftment of households be they from rural or urban settlements. Credit promotes capital investment and adoption of new technology, leading ultimately to better standards of life due to increased production and income.[2] Microfinance is a novel way to extend credit to the poor. Microfinance through SHGs has been recognised as one of the effective tools of poverty alleviation in almost all countries including India.[3]

Credit for women is a concept that has come to India only in the late 1980s. One novel solution has been group lending with joint liability. Group credit schemes involve borrowers to form homogeneous groups, which reduce transaction costs both for the lender and the borrower. Group credit also reduces monitoring costs by involving group members to monitor loan usage and repayment. If any member defaults, it leads to denial of further credit to the group members. However, joint asset management is a risky concept as there is no ownership by individuals who ensure proper use and repair of assets. Group lending has proved that credit worthiness is critical in reducing default risk. However, group formation risks are high and a period of loan amortisation is needed for better repayment.[4] The sample study on SHG members provides insight to the matter that credit and asset building process is an outcome of necessity. The present chapter prioritises discussion on source and purpose of credit, asset possession and structure of the SHG members in the Enclave and Peripheral Villages.

Credit Structure and Source

Table 6.1 shows credit structure of the sample members after joining the SHG. Sample members of 80.37 per cent have availed the credit, which include 82.69 per cent and 78.26 per cent in the Enclave and Peripheral Villages respectively (see Fig. 6.1). The Enclave settlement being highly urban in nature pressurise for the credit, as there is no substituting to it in any other form. The Peripheral settlement, no doubt, demand for the credit but there are alternatives available to them. The socio-cultural composition at times rescues the natives as life is taken as an easy going process. Contrary to this, the lives are not smooth and simple in the Enclave settlement and threatened by urban pressure and competition.

Table 6.1: Credit Status of the Sample SHG Members

Credit	*Enclave Villages*		*Peripheral Villages*		*Total*	
	No.	*%*	*No.*	*%*	*No.*	*%*
Not Availed	18	17.31	25	21.74	43	19.63
Availed	86	82.69	90	78.26	176	80.37
Total	**104**	**100.00**	**115**	**100.00**	**219**	**100.00**

Source: Field Survey, 2008.

Table 6.2 depicts that among the members who have availed credit from different sources. Only a thin per cent of

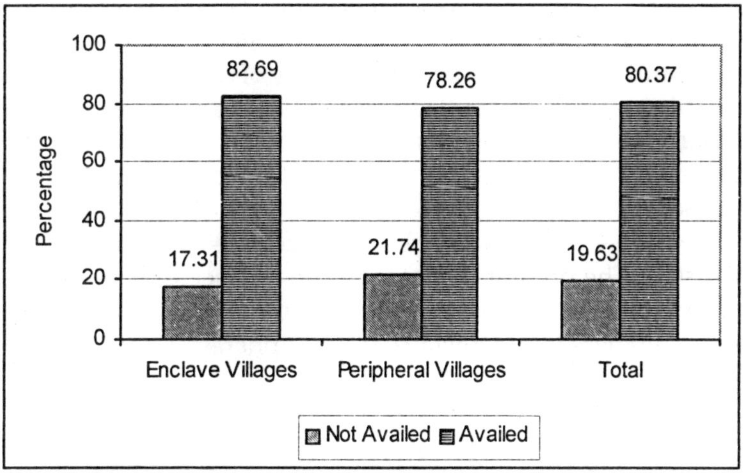

Fig. 6.1: Credit Status of the Sample SHG Members

Table 6.2: Sources of Credit to the Sample SHG Members

Source of Credit	*Enclave Villages*		*Peripheral Villages*		*Total*	
	No.	*%*	*No.*	*%*	*No.*	*%*
Relatives	—	—	3	3.33	3	1.70
Bank	3	3.49	7	7.78	10	5.68
SHG (Intra Group)	64	74.42	51	56.67	115	65.34
Both Bank & SHG	19	22.09	29	32.22	48	27.27
Total	**86**	**100.00**	**90**	**100.00**	**176**	**100.00**

Source: Field Survey, 2008.

members (1.70) has been found to have borrowed from relatives and friends followed by 5.68 per cent of members who have availed credit from single source, i.e., bank. However, a large section of members (65.34 per cent) has availed credit from intra-group funds. Almost 27.27 per cent members have availed credit from double sources, such as SHGs and banks (see Fig. 6.2). There are no instances of borrowing by the members from either relatives or friends in the Enclave settlement. Of the total credit services extended to the members, 74.42 per cent members have availed it from the intra-group sources and rest is from both bank and SHGs (25.58 per cent). In the

Peripheral settlement, 56.67 per cent of members have availed credit from the intra-group sources and 40 per cent from both bank and SHGs. At times, the relatives often help them, who constitute 3.33 per cent of the members in the Peripheral Villages.

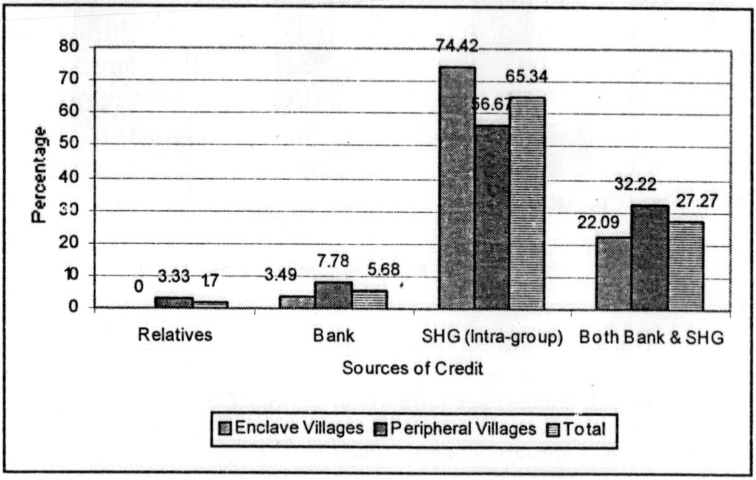

Fig. 6.2: Sources of Credit to the Sample SHG Members

The possible explanation for the present pattern of credit sources may be presented as follows:

(i) A large section of people at the grassroots are in dire need of financial assistance. The field survey of the SHG members of Enclave and Peripheral Villages provides knowledge that the members of SHGs needed financial help from the sources available to them. A large chunk of credit has been taken from the intra-group sources. This proves the fact that SHG stands as the bedrock of the fund savings and its mobilisation. This is a vital step towards self empowerment, a platform that keeps away from the misleading elements like the traditional money-lenders and economically influential people in the society, who, in fact exploit the poverty stricken masses to remain obedient to their commands and whims.

(ii) The SHGs have access to the formal financial institutions like Banks. This is an eye opening matter for the members to defend their financial crunch by getting the credit sanctioned. However, the percentage of members having access to the Banks is not so encouraging. But certainly, it is a step towards financial autonomy. The pressure from the people on government and participation by more number of banks through Public-Private Partnership (PPP) can help this cause.

(iii) There are a section of members who are yet to avail any credit. No group is actually homogeneous. This is an agglomeration of women who not only differ in their attitude but also in the socio-economic position. The new groups are yet to build their strength to accommodate all the members together. Members have to wait for their turn too. The SHGs have to wait for their own capacity building in order to get financial help from the financial institution like Banks.

(iv) In the Peripheral settlement, the SHGs are quite old. This provides advantage; first, the group capacity is high to accommodate the credit requirement of the members, second, it builds confidence with the financial institutions. In addition, there is scope for the credit from the relatives, friends and neighbours. Thereby, members need not depend too much on single source. In the Enclave settlement, SHG's role is high as members depend entirely on the performance of the group. There is very little scope for the members to approach for the credit from sources like relatives, friends and neighbours. They are yet to build strength of the groups.

Purpose of Credit

The purpose of loan is very basic to the needs of household. Microfinance involves financing for SHGs. Scarce resources and more demand for credit compels the group to make appropriate decision. The working fund grows with time and the group can build confidence of FIs for credit. On the whole, group is liable for the amount borrowed from the bank and responsible for monitoring the members and for taking rational decision to extend credit for the members. The sole motive is to avoid any misuse of fund. There are situations, where requirements of credit may not have single purpose or dominated by a singular cause. The purposes of credit of households form a circle. There is a continuous demand for the credit as household members have multifarious requirements. Therefore, SHG is a boon for the poor.

Table 6.3 depicts the figure of members' purpose for availing the credit. Purposes are different. They may differ with time. Some purposes may occur suddenly. There may be a single purpose or more than one. The credit availed for one purpose may have also been spent on different ones. In the present sample study on SHG members, it is found that 31.82 per cent of members availed credit for more than one purpose, which includes 23.26 per cent and 40 per cent in the Enclave and Peripheral Villages respectively. When 22.17 per cent of members availed credits for social purposes, it is as high as 27.91 per cent in the Enclave Villages compared to 16.66 per cent in the Peripheral Villages. Almost 11.93 per cent members availed loan for the housing purposes. Of them, 16.28 per cent belong to Enclave settlement and 7.78 per cent to the Peripheral settlement. There was demand for the business; 11.93 per cent of members opted for this. In the Enclave Villages, it is nearly 13.95 per cent, which is higher than that of Peripheral Villages (10 per cent). Of the 8.52 per cent of members who availed credit for the cattlehead purposes, 15.56 per cent are from the Peripheral Villages. Similarly, of the 8.52 per cent of members who asked for the credit for subsistence, household expenses and paying back old debts, 10.46 per cent and 6.67 per cent are respectively from the Enclave and Peripheral Villages. The purpose of household durables also finds place in availing the credit by the members (5.11 per cent) (see Fig. 6.3). This includes 6.98 per cent and 3.33 per cent from the Enclave and Peripheral Villages respectively.

Table 6.3: Purpose of Credit by the Sample SHG Members

Purpose of Credit	*Enclave Villages*		*Peripheral Villages*		*Total*	
	No.	*%*	*No.*	*%*	*No.*	*%*
Subsistence/Household Expenses/Paying back old Debt	9	10.46	6	6.67	15	8.52
Buying a Plot/land/House Construction/Repair & Sanitation	14	16.28	7	7.78	21	11.93
Cattlehead/Shed/Feed	1	1.16	14	15.56	15	8.52
Household Durables	6	6.98	3	3.33	9	5.11
Social Purpose (Health/ Marriage/Education)	24	27.91	15	16.66	39	22.17
Business	12	13.95	9	10.00	21	11.93
More than One Purpose	20	23.26	36	40.00	56	31.82
Total	**86**	**100.00**	**90**	**100.00**	**176**	**100.00**

Source: Field Survey, 2008.

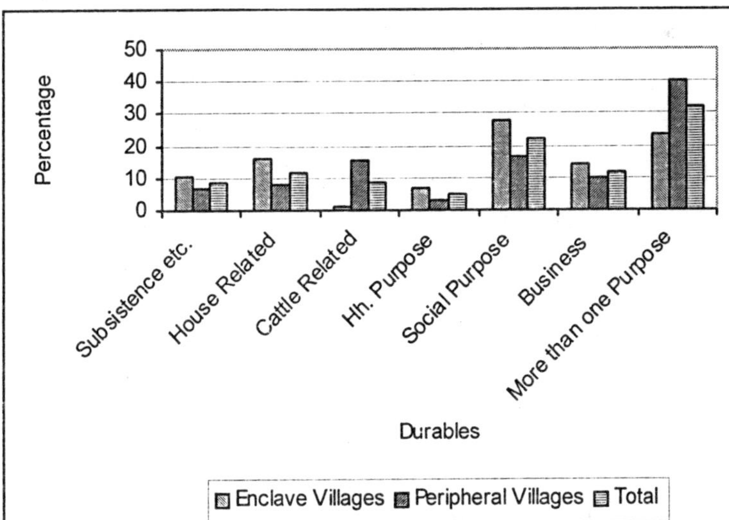

Fig. 6.3: Purpose of Credit by the Sample SHG Members

The possible reasons of difference and similarity may be because of the following factors:

(i) A large number of members availed loans either from

the groups or banks or both. This indicates the amount of success attached to the need and functioning of SHGs among the poor. This leads to independence and empowerment of neglected individuals in the society.

(ii) The loans had been availed by the members for all types of needs. The primary purpose of loans remained fulfilled without much struggle and effort that would have otherwise been riskier, costly and difficult, had these loans been fulfilled by the traditional moneylenders or from any other private sources.

(iii) In the urban settlements, members availed loans primarily for carrying out their social, housing, household expenses and business. The cattle purpose remains dominant in the Peripheral Villages along with credit for multiple purposes. The rural environment pulls towards plural activities. Organisational credit leads the members towards self-sufficiency and economic autonomy.

Average Annual Return

SHG forms a critical link for poor women to access a variety of financial services. SHG is an effective platform for women to participate in politics through awareness campaigns and community action. SHGs have also emerged as 'last mile' channels for government to distribute financial benefits and for corporations to retail their products through member-entrepreneurs. Even so, questions remain about the ability of SHGs to attain a primary objective, i.e., economic empowerment of poor women.[5] It is learnt that the income is generated through the interest charged from the intra-group members. The pooled funds are never kept idle, rather circulated along the line of requirement among the members. This process of intra-group borrowing solves two purposes; firstly, it is an easiest way to borrow money which fulfils the immediate requirement and this prevents any member from failing into the hands of moneylenders or similar; secondly, through the constant lending of money by the group at a very reasonable rate of interest, it generates income which is distributed to the members.

Table 6.4 presents the average annual return for the SHGs and the members. In the present sample study, the average annual return per group is Rs. 5,774. It is Rs. 5,461 in the Enclave settlements and Rs. 6,008 in the Peripheral settlements. The average annual return per member is Rs. 269, which is Rs. 282 and Rs. 306 in the Enclave and Peripheral Villages respectively.

Table 6.4: Average Annual Return (AAR)* of the Sample SHGs and Members in the Area of Study.

Area of Study	*AAR per Group* (Amount in Rs.)	*AAR per Member* (Amount in Rs.)
Enclave Villages	5,461	282
Peripheral Villages	6,008	306
Total	**5,774**	**296**

* Interest Charged from the Intra-group Credit.

Source: Field Survey, 2008.

The probable reasons of difference are assessed below:

(i) Return depends upon size (in terms of number of members in the group), volume (i.e. capital) and the input cost of the group. The older the group, higher is the size of capital. The return to the group is higher when it lends more money to the members. The Peripheral Villages have older groups and higher capital size compared to the Enclave Villages (see Tables 4.10 and 4.12). Therefore, the Peripheral Villages have better return than the Enclave Villages.

(ii) The return volume varies with the group because each group acts as a unit and the differences lie on the group size, bonus distribution frequency and overall activity of the group itself. The return is distributed equally among the members. No extra bonus is given to any of the members. Having more participation of members in terms of attending, conducting, managing the works of the SHG, etc. do not involve extra monetary benefit or award of extra bonus. Thus, members do hesitate to do the needful activities. However, everyone succumbs to the group's decision of equality to all circumstances as every member pays equal amount towards monthly thrift.

Impact Assessment

Table 6.5 highlights the possession of assets by the household of sample SHG members. Of the 94.06 per cent of households of SHG members who possess assets, 92.31 per cent of households are from Enclave Villages and 95.65 per cent are

Table 6.5: Assets Possessed by the Households of Sample SHG Members

Assets Status	*Enclave Villages*		*Peripheral Villages*		*Total*	
	No.	*%*	*No.*	*%*	*No.*	*%*
Having Assets	96	92.31	110	95.65	206	94.06
Not Having Assets	8	7.69	5	4.35	13	5.94
Total	**104**	**100.00**	**115**	**100.00**	**219**	**100.00**

Source: Field Survey, 2008.

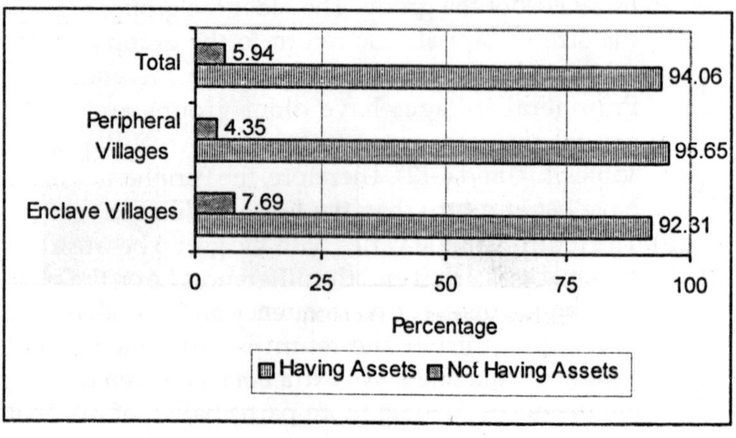

Fig. 6.4: Assets Possessed by the Sample Households

from the Peripheral Villages. A thin percentage of members (5.94) do not have assets in their house. This constitutes respectively 7.69 per cent and 4.35 per cent in the Enclave and Peripheral Villages (see Fig. 6.4). This fact is substantiated by the timing of accumulating assets.

Table 6.6 entails the timing of asset possession by the households of the sample SHG members from the pool of households having assets. In the sample, it is found that households of 63.11 per cent of members have had assets before joining the SHGs. The rest, *i.e.*, 36.89 per cent of member households accumulated assets after joining the SHGs. In the Enclave Villages, it is found that households of 69.79 per cent of members had assets before joining the SHGs. The remaining 30.21 per cent of member households accumulated assets after joining

Table 6.6: Timing of Assets' Possession by the Sample Households of SHG Members

Timing of Assets Possession	*Enclave Villages*		*Peripheral Villages*		*Total*	
	No.	*%*	*No.*	*%*	*No.*	*%*
Before Joining SHG	67	69.79	63	57.27	130	63.11
After Joining SHG	29	30.21	47	42.73	76	36.89
Total	**96**	**100.00**	**110**	**100.00**	**206**	**100.00**

Source: Field Survey, 2008.

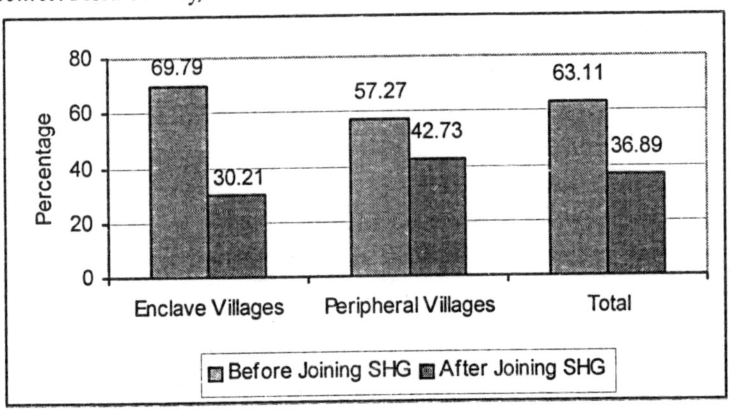

Fig. 6.5: Timing of Assets' Possession by the Sample Households of SHG Members

the SHGs. In the Peripheral Villages, it is found that households of 57.27 per cent of members had assets before joining the SHGs, while the remaining 42.73 per cent of member households accumulated assets after joining the SHGs (see Fig. 6.5).

The possible reasons of existing pattern may be attributed to the following factors:

(i) Almost 41 per cent of member households had no assets at the time of their entry to the SHGs. By the passage of time, 34.7 per cent of members have accumulated assets by availing loan from banks, groups or both sources. This, in fact, depicts the fact that SHGs are doing better work for the economic empowerment of sample members (see Tables 6.5 and 6.6).

(ii) There is a popular saying that 'unity is strength'. The groups became an easy source of strength at the grassroots, which not only facilitate funds from their savings but also acted as a platform of meetings, sharing of thoughts and misfortune and of planning to get rid of misfortune.

(iii) A number of households in the Enclave Villages had assets before joining the SHGs because of the compulsion of urban environment. Contrary to this, the households have done a lot after joining the group in the Peripheral settlements. The reason being they lacked access to procure funds. Availability of credit through SHG medium enhances the purchasing power of the household members, because of as its easy availability, flexibility in the repayment and requirements of no collateral.

Table 6.7 details about the asset categorisation of sample households after joining the SHGs. The picture about the possession of assets relates to the position after joining the SHGs. Out of the asset typology, cattleheads have been bought by 28.95 per cent of member households. Cattleheads are found with the households belonging to the Peripheral Villages (44.68

per cent). Of the 25 per cent of member households who have bought household assets like TV, refrigerator, etc., 37.93 per cent and 17.02 per cent are respectively from Enclave and Peripheral Villages. Of the 19.74 per cent of member households that have gone for land, house construction, sanitation related assets, 34.48 per cent and 10.64 per cent are from the Enclave and Peripheral settlements respectively. In addition, 26.32 per cent members have accumulated more than one asset, and this includes 24.14 per cent and 27.66 per cent members in the Enclave and Peripheral Villages respectively (see Fig. 6.6).

Table 6.7: Assets Procured in Households of the Sample SHG Members after Joining

Type of Assets	*Enclave Viliages*		*Peripheral Villages*		*Total*	
	No.	*%*	*No.*	*%*	*No.*	*%*
Land/Plot/House Construction/ Extension/Repair & Sanitation	10	34.48	5	10.64	15	19.74
Vehicle/ TV/Refrigerator/ Washing Machine/ Ornament/Bed/Swing/ Embroidery Machine etc.	11	37.93	8	17.02	19	25.00
Cattlehead	1	3.45	21	44.68	22	28.95
More than One Assets	7	24.14	13	27.66	20	26.32
Total	**29**	**100.00**	**47**	**100.00**	**76**	**100.00**

Source: Field Survey, 2008.

The following reasons may explain the present pattern:

(i) In the process of asset building, majority of members belonging to the Peripheral settlement have gone for cattleheads thinking that the dairy products have demand in Delhi market and also calves after milch process can be of a good maıket value. This kind of assets suits the rural environment, where space for domestication is not a problem along with readily available of fodder.

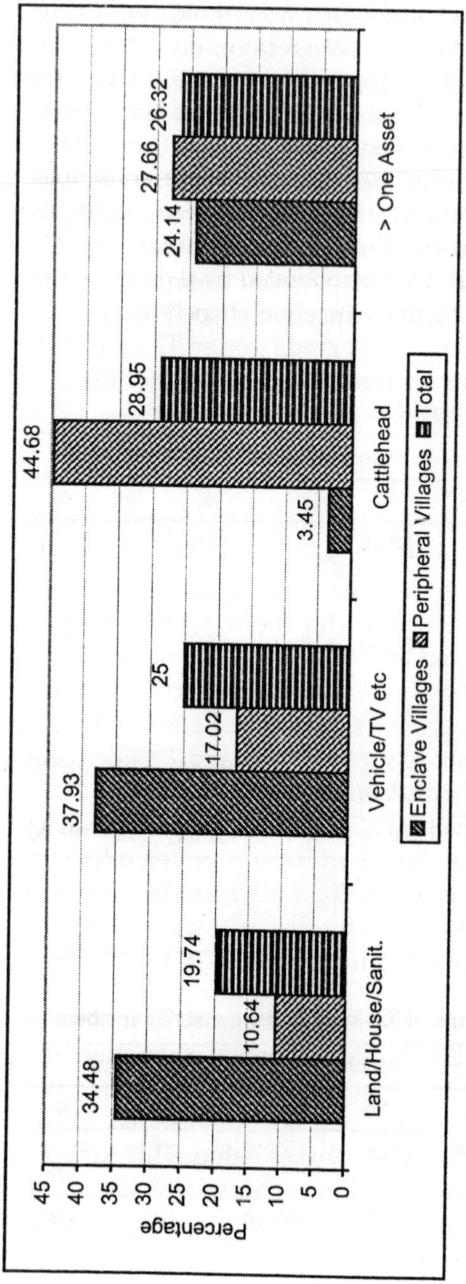

Fig. 6.6: Types of Assets Available in the Households of SHG Members

(ii) Among others, assets related to land for house, sanitation, etc. get priority as it is the most basic requirement for the family. In the Enclave Villages, the members have gone for it. In the urban space, to own house is a matter of difficult task.

(iii) No one asset can satisfy one's needs in the household. Wants and needs vary with time. If there were purchasing power with the people, they would end up buying the necessary things. This is corroborated by the findings in both types of settlements, where members have gone for more than one asset out of the credit money. This indicates that the availability of funds with SHGs and lending process have positive impact at the grassroots.

Attitudinal Impact

Table 6.8 highlights the remarks about the SHGs by the sample members. It is found that 91.32 per cent of members are satisfied with the working and functioning of the SHGs as against 8.68 per cent of members who are found not satisfied (see Fig. 6.7). Those satisfied are 90.38 per cent and 92.17 per cent in the Enclave and Peripheral Villages respectively. A few sample members (8.68 per cent) are not satisfied with the functioning of SHGs; they are 9.62 per cent and 7.83 per cent in the Enclave and Peripheral Villages respectively.

Table 6.9 shows the level of satisfaction by the sample SHG members who have been satisfied with the overall working of the SHGs. There are 41 per cent, 42.5 per cent and 16.5 per cent of satisfied members who express their view towards SHGs as good, very good and excellent respectively. In the Enclave

Table 6.8: Remarks about the SHGs by the Sample SHG Members

Satisfactory Remark	*Enclave Villages*		*Peripheral Villages*		*Total*	
	No.	*%*	*No.*	*%*	*No.*	*%*
Satisfied	94	90.38	106	92.17	200	91.32
Not Satisfied	10	9.62	9	7.83	19	8.68
Total	**104**	**100.00**	**115**	**100.00**	**219**	**100.00**

Source: Field Survey, 2008.

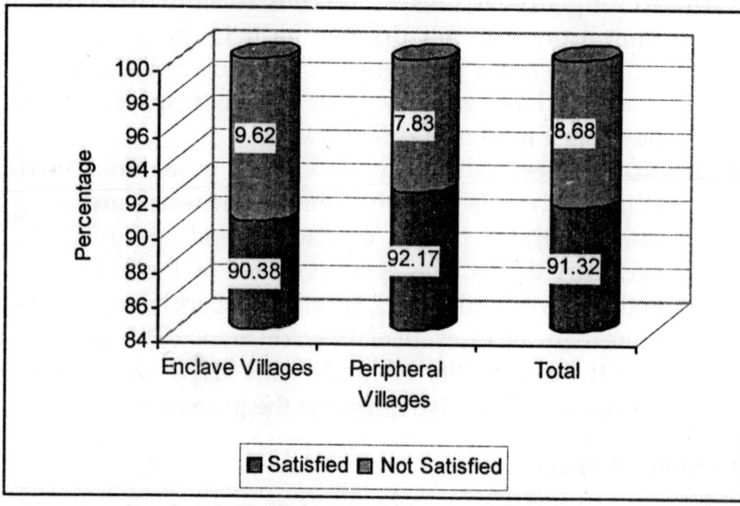

Fig. 6.7: Remark about the SHG by the Sample Members

Table 6.9: Level of Satisfaction by the Sample SHG Members

Level of Satisfaction	*Enclave Villages*		*Peripheral Villages*		*Total*	
	No.	*%*	*No.*	*%*	*No.*	*%*
Good	52	55.32	30	28.30	82	41.00
Very Good	31	32.98	54	50.94	85	42.50
Excellent	11	11.70	22	20.75	33	16.50
Total	**94**	**100.00**	**106**	**100.00**	**200**	**100.00**

Source: Field Survey, 2008.

Villages, the corresponding figures are respectively 55.32 per cent, 32.98 per cent and 11.70 per cent. However, in the Peripheral Villages, 28.3 per cent, 50.94 per cent and 20.75 per cent of satisfied members expressed their view towards SHGs as good, very good and excellent respectively (see Fig. 6.8).

The possible reasons may be adjudged as follows:

(i) The remark by someone about an event, organisation or individual speaks one's experience and association with them. The level of satisfaction varies from individual to individual. The realisation process depends on one's maturity and perception level. As any odd human grouping, the SHGs are run by the individual members. However, the level of satisfaction expressed speaks about their liking towards SHGs. Older the group, larger is the benefit to the group members in terms of access to the credit, capital and return. New groups are inexperienced and have to wait for the benefits from its capacity building. Their remark about the SHGs may differ from the senior members.

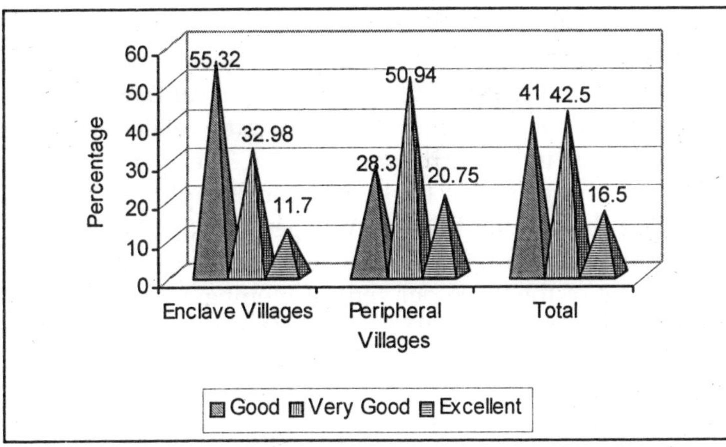

Fig. 6.8: Level of Satisfaction by the Sample SHG Members

(ii) In the Peripheral settlement, sample members speak high about the SHGs, and it is not so in the Enclave Villages. In Enclave Villages, the people have not properly understood the philosophy of SHG's *modus operandi* or still they need some time to properly assimilate to group activities. In the Peripheral Villages, the attitude towards SHG is better because people have time to spare for the growth of the SHGs. Higher the involvement higher is the value adjudgement.

To sum up, it can be stated that group credit plays an important role at the grassroots. Lack of adequate credit has remained a concern for the society. Of the members, 80.37 per cent have availed credit. It is 82.69 per cent and 78.26 per cent in the Enclave and Peripheral Villages respectively. There are 65.34 per cent of members who have availed credit from the intra-group itself. It is 74.42 per cent and 56.67 per cent in the Enclave and Peripheral Villages respectively. Relatives do not have much role in this aspect. It is non-existent in the Enclave Villages, while 3.33 per cent of members have availed credit from neighbours, relatives or friends in the Peripheral Villages. All the members of households have a good number of wants. There is, in fact, a purpose, which motivate them for drawing the credit. In this sample study, 31.82 per cent of members have multiple purposes for the credit. The social purpose has dominated in the Enclave Villages (27.91 per cent), while other than multiple purposes it is social and cattle related activities that dominated in the Peripheral Villages. The average annual return for the group is higher in the Peripheral Villages (Rs. 6,008) than in the Enclave Villages (Rs. 5,461). Similarly average annual return for the SHG members follows the same pattern. Out of the 94.06 per cent of members who have had assets, 92.31 per cent and 95.65 per cent are from the Enclave and Peripheral Villages respectively. Among the members having assets, 36.89 per cent accumulated assets after joining the group. It is 30.21 and 42.73 per cent in the Enclave and Peripheral Villages respectively. The typology of assets indicate that 44.68 per cent of members in the Peripheral Villages have gone for the cattleheads, whereas 37.93 per cent of members have gone for the accumulation of household durable assets in the Enclave Villages. The SHGs' functioning has been appreciated by the opinions of the members. Above 90 per cent members are satisfied with the SHGs' functioning. However, among them, 41 per cent, 42.5 per cent and 16.5 per cent of members have remarked it is good, very good and excellent.

NOTES

1. N. Lalith and R. Dayanandan (2005): *NABARD and Rural*

Transformation. New Delhi: Dominant Publishers and Distributors, pp. 1-2.

2. K. Vatta (2003): 'Microfinance and Poverty Alleviation', *Economic and Political Weekly*, Vol. XXXVIII, No. 5, p. 432.
3. S. Borbora and R. Mahanta (2001): 'Micro Credit through Self-Help Groups and Its Impact: A Case of Rastriya Gramin Bank Vikas Nidhi Credit and Saving Programme in Assam', *Indian Journal of Agricultural Economics*, Vol. 56, No. 3, p. 449.
4. K.G. Karmakar (1999): *Rural Credit and Self-Help Groups: Microfinance Needs and Concepts in India*. New Delhi: Sage Publications, p. 171.
5. *http://www.microfinancegateway.org/content/article/detail/49567*

7

Microfinance and Empowerment: Role of NGOs

Empowerment is a relative concept, meaning that it depends upon the process and nature of disempowerment. In a class society the workers may talk of disempowerment while the gender specialists would view it from the point of gender[1] discrimination. The race and caste concepts would look at it from the point of view of biological as well as social discrimination, while for the advocates of identity politics it would mean claiming own identity from the oppressor. "Empowerment and inclusion are often seen as a complementary process, empowerment focussing on enhancing various capabilities of the excluded groups, while inclusive policies create enabling environment at the system's levels for the excluded groups to enjoy their rights."[2] Empowerment process has three dimensions such as economic, social and political that supports each other. Economic dimension includes access to and command over tangible and intangible assets; social aspects comprise changing the existing discriminatory ideology and culture; and political front takes account of increase in the presence and influence in the power structure.[3]

The persistence of the female-male gaps in human development in India is definitely indicative of the low status assigned to women in the Indian social system. This is obvious from the findings that fewer females than males are involved in waged labour, are literate and participate in the electoral process in India. Further, the structural processes of kinship structures, development and social stratification interact with each other to affect women's status differently in different parts of India.[4] Towards empowerment of women, a lot of initiatives have been carried out by the women's movement and a wide-spread network of NGOs, which have strong grassroots presence and deep insight into and focus on women's concern.[5] Microfinance programmes have the potential to transform power relations and empower the poor – both men and women.[6]

Defining the Concept 'NGO'

The definition of Voluntary Organisations has been a matter of great debate and controversy for social scientists. However, besides defining them, some terms have also been used such as P.A. (Private Agencies, an American term), N.G.O. (Non-Governmental Organisation, a UN term in its charter's Article 71), N.P.P.F. (Non-Party Political Formation) and V.A. (Voluntary Agencies). NGO is popularly used term which logically excludes governmental and quasi-governmental agencies and entire organised sector of economy.[7] A 'Voluntary Organisation' is defined as "a group of persons organised on the basis of voluntary membership without state control for furtherance of some common interest of its members."[8] By its definition, voluntary action suggests doing something without looking for personal gain. The scope for voluntary action is, therefore, unbounded.[9] In its simplest form, an NGO is a body of people who come together to provide help to those who fail to accumulate sufficient resources to survive. In its most ambitious form, an NGO is a private, not-for-profit institution dedicated to influencing the working structure of government and ensure the greater welfare of all citizens.[10]

The concept of NGOs is too narrow because it includes only organisations that are explicitly involved in the promotion of social and economic development. Depending on a particular observer's definition of 'development', the category of 'NGO' may exclude or include schools, universities, hospitals, social clubs, professional associations, social welfare agencies, religious groups, and cultural institutions—all of which would naturally be considered integral parts of the non-profit sector in most parts of the world. 'NGO' thus becomes a term of approbation carrying ideological baggage rather than a neutral term that can reliably be used for description and analysis.[11]

In most developing countries, there is no congruence between the recipient system and the delivery system. This is because of the failure to mobilise the poor to demand service and to obtain help from the government. In the absence of effective organisations, the poor have not been able to obtain their due share from the developmental programmes. There is, therefore, need for an effective micro-level institutional arrangements to involve the people in developmental programmes. Now, the general acceptance is that NGOs provide an effective micro-level institutional arrangement.[12]

There is no universal classification system of NGOs. They could be grouped on their relationship with the state, operating philosophy, advocacy issues, target groups etc. United Nations (UN) clearly specifies that an NGO must be independent from the direct control of any government. There are a few key characteristics of NGOs. An NGO is (i) independent of government control, (ii) a private organisation, (iii) not constituted as a political party, (iv) a non-profit-making organisation, (v) essentially non-violent, and (vi) broadly geared towards improving/changing the existing conditions of the society.[13]

Salamon and Anheier (1994) define 'NGO' as an organisation possessing the following six attributes. They are (1) non-governmental, (2) non-profit-making, (3) voluntary, (4) of a solid and continuing form, (5) altruistic, and (6) philanthropic. The term 'non-governmental' means that an NGO must carry out its decision-making as an organisation independently from the wishes of the government. To be 'non-profit-making' means its activities must not be driven by profit-making motives. 'Voluntary' means the only qualification for membership must be desire of an individual to participate.

Condition 'of a solid and continuing form' means NGO must be an on-going entity with solid organisational form. 'Altruistic' means the immediate purpose of an NGO is to act for the benefit of others. The last requirement, 'philanthropic' means an NGO has a poor prospect of receiving adequate payments from the recipients of its services. This requirement is predicted on the fact that the recipients of services offered by the NGOs in developing countries are socially and economically disadvantaged. As a consequence, NGOs must raise funds for their activities from sources other than the recipients. The foregoing six requirements may be satisfied simultaneously only by archetypal NGOs. The NGOs in actual existence may diverge from the archetypal models to some extent.[14]

The State, People and NGOs

The state in developing countries like India has the greatest responsibility to bring about planned socio-economic development and nation building. The state is not an end in itself but a means to an end and that end is to promote all-round, balanced, integrated development of all citizens and the nation as a whole.[15] The civil society manifests itself through myriads of households, communities, associations, voluntary groups of different hues and kinds, social service workers, non-profit organisations cooperatives, unions, women's development groups and environmental NGOs. Not only does it have its definite place in modern state but also performs vital functions for its members through the network of these institutions.[16]

The philosophy on which the NGOs have supported by the Government of India since independence is *Sarvodaya* and *Gramodaya*. During the period of Sixth Five-Year Plan (1980-85), the Planning Commission recognised the achievements of NGOs and sought to work through them formally.[17] During the Seventh Five-Year Plan (1985-90), the Government was serious to involve voluntary organisations in various developmental programmes particularly in the rural development.[18] It had emphasised the need to closely associate

NGOs with rural developmental programmes, particularly poverty alleviation. In the Eighth Five-Year Plan (1992-97), the role of voluntary agencies has been defined as "providing a basis for innovation with new approach towards integrated development, ensuring feedback regarding impact of various programmes and securing the involvement of local communities, particularly, those below the poverty line."[19] In the Ninth Five-Year Plan (1997-2002), both Integrated Rural Development Programme (IRDP) and *Swarnajayanti Gram Swarozgar Yojana* (SGSY) were subsidy-driven programmes. This subsidy itself had become major obstacle in the promotion of self-employment venture, which has been rhetoric in the Tenth Five-Year Plan (2002-07). The scope of NGOs was further expanded considering their services rendered to the poor in the rural areas.[20]

Though the government made efforts to establish a 'shadow state'[21] soon after independence, it gained momentum only with the introduction of economic reforms, prescriptions to reduce the government role in social sector development and a decline in the budget for social sector. Over time, the government gradually transferred the responsibility of social services to the NGOs. The NGOs, therefore, were expected to assume greater role in providing social services.[22]

Despite NGO weaknesses such as spatial limitations, allegation on their accountability and constraints in working at micro levels, they have been gaining importance in service delivery and have become a prominent member of civil society. This has resulted in the proliferation of NGOs, diversification and multiplication of their activities and rapid flow of resources from government and donors.[23] Voluntary effort will no doubt continue to grow in the coming years but it can accelerate if the environment is more congenial to its growth. If the professional and managerial capabilities of voluntary organisations are built up in a systematic manner they can make tremendous contributions in bringing about people's participation both in financial terms and through participatory support.[24]

The Government officials perceive poverty to be the

inability to access basic needs due to low income. In contrast, the NGOs have wider perception of poverty that includes vulnerability, powerlessness, isolation and assetlessness. NGOs emphasize on building of the organisations of the poor through process-oriented approach and strengthen their institutional capacity to address the root cause of poverty. The Government officials, on the other hand, adopt target-oriented approach to form a large number of groups in short space of time to quickly scale up the activities for visible impact.[25]

In the context of developments in Afghanistan, it has been argued that there is a danger that as NGOs try to negotiate spaces with different strongmen who control the development structure of a state, they in fact end up severely compromised. Therefore, NGOs are not considered the panacea for the intractable problems of development of a state.[26]

NGOs that were initially small have grown in size, budgets and areas of operation, programmes and funding. NGOs have come to occupy the centre state in the sphere of development since 1980s, which is often referred as 'the NGO decade in development'. Many international agencies like the World Bank, which were earlier working exclusively through national governments, find NGOs now as a dependable force which may be involved in implementing some of their projects.[27]

It is observed that during past few decades NGOs are becoming increasingly important in the people-oriented development programmes and projects at the grassroots level by virtue their involvement and commitment to the rural poor. The success and failure of the NGOs are greatly dependent on the attitudes of the Government Officials (GOs) in the areas of operation on the one hand and rigid/dynamic policy framework on the other. Under facilitating condition, with proper guidance and direction, the NGOs are expected to perform better as compared to other organisations. The openness, clear objectives and methods of operations and targets are expected from the NGOs to avail protection and guarantees from the Government Officials in order to function better in the rural areas for the poor. So the GOs and NGOs should be conceived as the two important developments, entrepreneurs-*cum*-partners,in the development game, and not as competitors. The activities and methods of operations of both the organisation/agencies should be properly coordinated and integrated to harvest the most meaningful results. In the training environment, both groups should be brought together for mutual benefits, common agreements and identifying common goals and strategies of development for the rural poor.[28]

Space for NGOs in the State

Social Space

When the systems of market, state and community fail to perform their resource-distributing functions properly, there is room for NGOs to emerge as a fourth category of agents to distribute resources on their own[29] or to interfere with the existing distribution systems, making up for or correcting their shortcomings[30] (see Fig. 7.1).

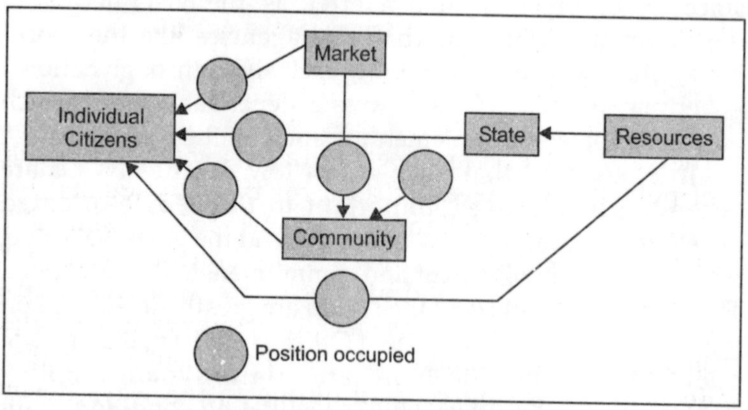

Source: Shigetomi (2002:10).

Fig. 7.1: The Space for NGOs in the Society

Economic Space

Assuming that the large triangle represents the total volume of resources required by an individual economy, Figure 7.1

describes the situation where the market, the state and communities each satisfies some portions of the total demand, when there is space left uncovered by these existing sectors, an arena emerges in which NGOs can act. We can call this an economic space for NGOs. A large economic space means that the services of NGOs are in great demand[31] (see Fig. 7.2).

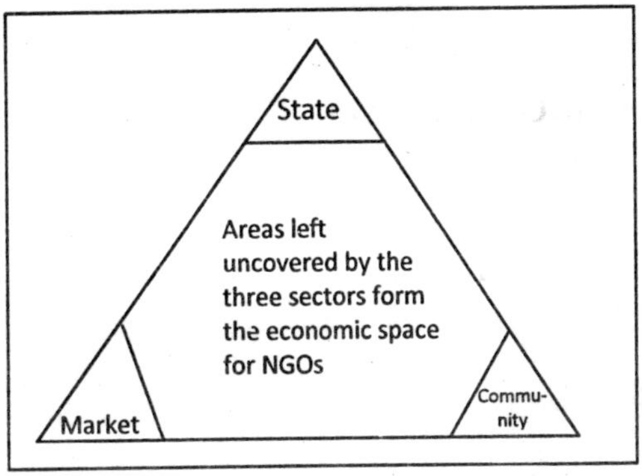

Source: Shigetomi (2002:12).

Fig. 7.2: The Economic Space for NGOs

Political Space

The way NGOs exist and operate in a given country is the extent of political control exercised over them by the state and society."[32] "NGOs will target their own action mainly at the state, because it is often much more difficult to change the market artificially, and also because resources held by communities are often far smaller than those controlled by the state. It is never certain that the government will make its decisions on resource distribution in the ways deemed desirable by NGOs. In order to address this question, NGOs may try to change the political and administrative decision-making process themselves, by staging a campaign for better politics. This is a direction pursued by NGOs towards reform. Better politics here means the existence and functioning of a mechanism by which the political will and opinions exercised by the people are transmitted to the government[33] (see Fig. 7.3).

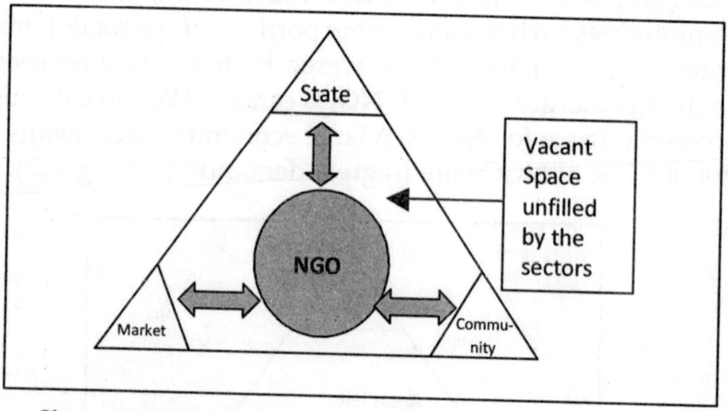

Source: Shigetomi (2002:16)

Fig. 7.3: The Political Space for NGOs

NGOs and SHGs

India has been experimenting since 1960s with flexible systems, giving a lot of freedom to the NGOs to set up SHGs. The Tenth Five-Year Plan (2002-07) states that "the innovative experiments and alternative models developed in the voluntary sector are rich and diverse and also worth replicating. These efforts have often demonstrated the success of alternative models in the areas of credit, awareness generation, organising women into SHGs, self-employment, etc. RMK is a success story of reaching microcredit to the poor and assetless women in the informal sector through the medium of voluntary organisations."[34]

One of the important strategies of the NGOs was the formation and promotion of SHGs (Photograph 7.1). The NGOs, which combined empowerment and development component in their work sought to build people's institutions based on self-help and establish linkages with government departments with a view to either tapping the resources or changing state-led development paradigm by involving the government machinery in the process.[35]

Innovative and cost effective models of NGOs would attract the government development machinery towards them in jointly undertaking the development work. Even some NGOs have developed innovative and people-centred approach in the identification of the poor, formation and development of SHGs in microfinance. Attracted by these approaches, banks established interface with SHGs under NABARD's programme.[36]

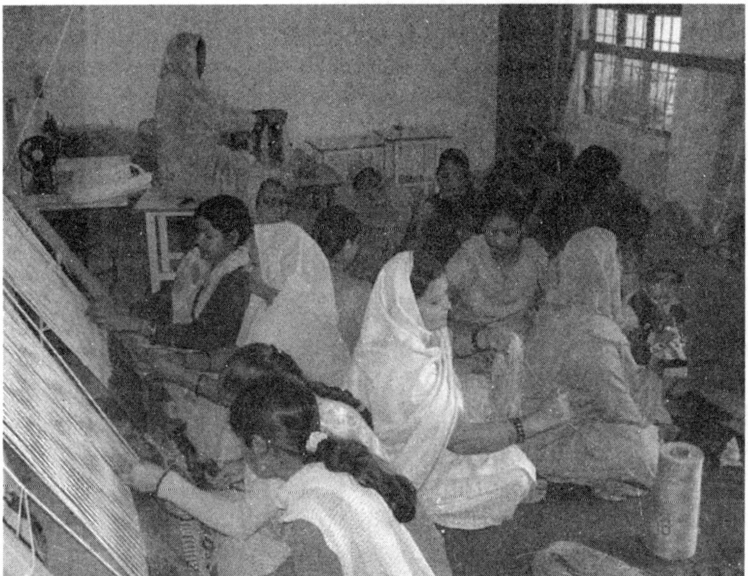

Photograph 7.1: Members of SHGs receive Training at the MRYDO Office Building

A pilot project for linking SHGs with banks was introduced in 1992 by NABARD[37] to encourage thrift and savings among the rural poor and to supplement their credit needs through the banking system. The project has the following main features:

- The VAs/NGOs and other Self-Help Promotional Institutions (SHPIs) including a few banks who play the role of facilitator.
- SHGs should be in existence for at least six months actively promoting savings and lending among their members.

- SHGs are normally informal groups.
- The size of the group is not to exceed 20.
- Banks will finance the SHGs in promotion to the savings mobilised by the group. The proportion of savings to loan could vary from 1:1 to 1:4 depending on the assessment by the bank.

NABARD's target for coverage of SHGs during the year 1999-2000 was 50,000 SHGs and one million SHGs by 2008.

Relevance of NGOs

Women belonging to the deprived sections of society have limited access to resources or employment opportunities. They live in conditions that do not allow them to meet bare consumption needs. They do not have control on even the money earned by them from hard physical labour. Institutional credit is difficult to access as women rarely have any property rights to mortgage or collateral to offer. They have to depend on moneylenders for their production-*cum*-consumption needs. This brings them to fall into a vicious cycle of perpetual poverty and indebtedness. In patriarchy, the men do not welcome NGOs/SHGs working for the upliftment of women, as an economically independent woman is perceived as a threat to their male dominance. That a woman's savings/earnings are generally used for the family is hardly remembered.[38]

NGOs involved in forming women SHGs should have knowledge and expertise in education, rural health and hygiene, tribal development, etc. A large number of case studies on women SHGs and their association with the group reveal that individually these women had accepted their poverty and miseries as due to divine fate or destiny and had little hope of improving their lot in life. But the formation of SHGs has led to growing awareness; education and availability of information led to confidence building and the ability to handle complex issues. The very same women who were not able to deal with banks, government officials and NGOs, are now very successful.[39] Various case studies in Orissa show that there is a positive correlation between credit availability and women's empowerment.

SHGs set up by NGOs, with the assistance of bank linkage, ensure individual loans for women beneficiaries and structure and fix individual/joint liability for repayment. There is little stress on asset creation and more on production-*cum*-consumption loans, ensuring quicker repayment and less borrower fatigue in loan repayment. The rate of repayment is much higher in SHGs as there is no subsidy involved in it.[40] Credit groups should be allowed to come up on their own or through the intervention of NGOs rather than being formed by financing agencies. If the group takes the shape and strength of its own, group dynamics ensures that group solidarity and group consciousness are fostered.[41] SHGs evolve flexible systems of operations; often with the help of NGOs, they manage common pooled resources in a democratic manner.[42]

The staff from the Grama Vikas, an NGO working with SHGs in Kolar District of Karnataka, attends the meetings regularly if the group happened to be young and inexperienced. In the case of older groups, the staff attends one meeting in a month. It may be noted here that MRYDO (like Grama Vikas in Karnataka) has been following a withdrawal strategy wherein the role of the organisation gradually becomes only facilitative. As a part of this strategy, the organization constantly monitors the status of SHGs. If the monitoring reveals that the group attained self-management capacity, the staff would not spend much time on basic aspects like facilitating the group meetings, etc. However, in the villages where there is a problem of finding a book-writer either from among members or from the village, the staff continues to play an active role in the preparation and maintenance of accounts and documents relating to the SHG.[43]

There are a large number of NGOs that have undertaken the task of financial intermediation. Majority of these NGOs are registered as trust or society. Many NGOs felt that combining financial intermediation with their core competency activity of social intermediation is not the right path. Therefore, they have been performing non-financial functions like socio-cultural and capacity building activities, facilitate training of SHGs, undertake internal audit, promote new groups, etc.[44]

Some NGOs working with marginalized sections typically do so with a conception of benefits rather than rights. The functioning methodology of NGOs, in many cases, is project based and they are engaged with time-bound programmes of opportunity creation in specific spheres. In addition, most NGOs work closely with and are dependent for funding upon state agencies, international development agencies and multilateral organisations.[45]

SHG-Bank Linkage

While SHG linkage has the capacity to develop into an alternative credit delivery system, the problem is of finding an adequate number of committed bankers and NGOs to carry forward this programme.[46] My personal encounter with the group members and staff of the MRYDO unveils the fact that there is a greater demand for the banks to provide the loan but banks remain unheard about it even if the applications have been submitted quite early (Photograph 7.2).

Photograph 7.2: Distribution of Bank Loan among the SHG Members at Shiv Enclave, Delhi

Banks have been apathetic to SHGs linkage partly because the concept has yet to percolate to the branch level with each bank having its own guidelines. Also, SHG lending is not perceived as normal lending activity, but treated as a concessional dispensation. Most bankers distrust lending to the poor and to NGOs due to the poor credibility of existing poverty alleviation programmes and poor interaction between NGOs and banks. On their part, NGOs also distrust banks and their bureaucratic procedures. Most NGOs are not interested in thrift-based programmes as they depend upon foreign funding on very generous terms and without much interference. Many NGOs feel that expert manpower is needed for maintaining thrift-based programmes especially keeping accounts. But, the major problem is that of linkage with banks due to the suspicious attitude of bankers as they are handling the money of other people.[47] However, as microfinance is growing, which is estimated to have a Rs. 60,000 crore market, a number of private equities and venture capital firms have now started training their attention at, and a few top private banks taking special interest.[48]

The emergence of SHGs as a supplementary credit channel and its evolution from a pilot project to a business opportunity for the banks is a departure from traditional banking practices. This has necessitated constant review of the functioning of SHGs and assessment of their strength and weaknesses. The flexibility provided in operations and in the linkage process has encouraged and helped the groups/NGOs/Banks to evolve procedures and patterns suitable to their needs (Photograph 7.3). This needs to be continued. At the same time, standardisation may be attempted only in areas where flexibility has been misinterpreted or where imposition or rigidity is necessary.[49] The record keeping and accounting procedures maintained at the SHG and NGO level varied depending upon the involvement of the NGO, level of awareness of members, etc. There is no need to impose a common system for the sake of uniformity. Most of the bankers were of the view that the transaction costs for SHGs were low compared to those for small loans by banks, especially when the linkage was through an NGO.[50]

Photograph 7.3: A Buffalo was bought through Intra-group Lending in the Village Kheda Dabar, Delhi

In the Urban Context

NGOs around the world have led the campaign to expand banking services to the poor. There are many successful examples of microcredit programmes in rural India, but few have had a specific focus on urban India. The urban poor are indeed borrowing for uses that are covered by the Government's Urban Poverty Alleviation Initiatives (UPAIs), such as housing, health, childcare and education. But the fact that NGO-led microcredit schemes have succeeded where government schemes have failed, is recognition that the former's programmes have been better at addressing the problems. The experiences of successful NGOs like MRYDO show that the poor are bankable. It illustrates that microcredit can be used as a core instrument of empowerment for the urban poor. When used in conjunction with other programmes, it actually serves to improve the quality of life of the urban poor. The method of administration of this credit also plays a role in its effectiveness.[51]

Table 7.1: Promotion of SHGs by MRYDO

Sl. No.	*Agencies*	*No. of SHGs Promoted*
1.	NABARD	81
2.	DCW	34
3.	RMK	20
4.	GRC	30
5.	Own Initiative	91
	Total	**256**

Source: MRYDO Record.

In group-lending programmes, the functions of screening, monitoring and enforcement of repayment, to a large extent, are transferred from the bank's agent to the borrowers, that is, the group members themselves. Compared with socially and physically distant bank agents, group members can perform all such functions more effectively and at a lower cost. The group members are able to access complex and sensitive information just like informal lenders. Transaction costs are thus reduced. The mismatch between demand and supply is minimised because the grou uses the money according to its own needs. Flexibility of loan repayment is also enhanced, as the repayment schedule of the individual to the group need not match that of the group to the bank. It is not the rigidity of banks but their constraints due to high transaction costs and risks because of asymmetric information, that they cannot extend such credit to individual borrowers.[52]

Table 7.2: Some Facts and Figures about SHGs by the Initiative of MRYDO

Sl. No.	*Parameters*	*Dec.1999 to June 2004*	*Oct. 2005 to Oct. 2008*
1.	Opening of Bank A/c by SHGs	84	75
2.	Total Saving	Rs.27,64,650	Rs.32,93,100
3.	Total Internal Loaning	Rs.79,22,750	Rs.89,26,900
4.	Total Loan Recovered	Rs.53,05,650	Rs.55,38,900
5.	Total Outstanding Loan	Rs.26,17,100	Rs.30,30,900
6.	Credit Amount of Linkage	Rs.31,55,000	Rs.11,29,000

Source: MRYDO Record.

With Reference to MRYDO

Model Rural Youth Development Organisation (MRYDO) is a registered NGO working in Najafgarh (South-West Delhi) for the last 14 years (registered in August 1995). The approach of the NGO is participatory (Photograph 7.4). Along with other activities, the NGO has been concentrating in the field of SHGs in collaboration with NABARD, RMK, DCW and GRC. This is one of the pioneer organisations to link SHGs with nationalised banks in Delhi. Till now the MRYDO has been able to promote 256 SHGs covering 5120 women in different locations in Delhi (see Table 7.1). More than 150 SHGs have been linked with SBI, CBI and Allahabad Bank availing loan worth more than Rs. 175 lakhs and repayment is 100 per cent (see Table 7.2).

Photograph 7.4: Author with the Director of MRYDO, Najafgarh, Delhi

The Impact *per se*

The role of NGOs in mobilising savings and distributing credit in the rural areas is well known. Many of them have done commendable work in the rural areas compared to other formal institutions.[53] The country-wide network of more than 12,000 Voluntary Organisations have been playing a very significant role in the empowerment of women and development of children as they share the major burden of implementing Governmental policies and programmes. Their initiatives have often proved to be successful alternatives in the areas of women's literacy, support services, microcredit for poor women, employment and income generation, gender sensitisation, organising women into SHGs and fight against atrocities on women and the girl child, etc.[54]

The impact of SHGs has relatively been more pronounced on social aspects than on the economic aspects.[55] Emancipation of women is an essential prerequisite for economic development and social progress of the nation. One of the major contributions of microfinance is towards women's empowerment (Photograph 7.5). It is revealed that SHGs are really a boon in the rural areas, which gives financial autonomy to the rural women and makes them economically independent.[56] As women's groups exclusively dominate the SHGs, their empowerment both on the economic and social fronts is one of the greatest opportunities in the mainstream of developmental activities (Photograph 7.6). Opportunities for earning through deposits and higher off-farm activities improve their disposable income.[57] Consequently, family income too will substantially increase. Apart from economic changes, there are tremendous social changes too. The women command more respect, get their due affection and rightful place in the family. Their involvement in family decisions has been substantially enhanced. As a group, women have gained more confidence and power. This ultimately leads them towards empowerment.[58] In addition to meeting financial requirements, the SHG has become a platform for exchange of experiences and ideas beyond social participation by members, especially women.[59] The SHGs are making the process of development participatory and democratic and are displaying their sustainability even in the absence of any subsidy.[60]

Photograph 7.5: The Tailoring Business of an SHG Member in the Surakhpur Village, Delhi

Photograph 7.6: A Member of SHG owns a Beauty Parlour at Jhoroda Village, Delhi – A Step towards Women's Empowerment

However, interventions by NGOs in themselves are too small to make a significant difference in the national context. While there is a national policy to support priority sector lending and some schemes have begun to partner credit with training and group action, what is missing is a national institution responsible for really pushing the partnership of urban microcredit and self-help across India's cities. A very important step towards making credit the core component is the creation of an Apex Bank for Urban Development. An apex bank's role could be to act as a nodal national-level agency for urban microcredit, learning in part from the success of NABARD's experience in rural microcredit.[61]

To sum up, it is to be mentioned that empowerment focuses on enhancing various capabilities of the marginalized groups. There is persistent gap between male and female indicating low status assigned to the women. An NGO is a body of people who come together to provide help to those who fail to accumulate sufficient resources to survive. Over the time, the government gradually transferred the responsibility of social services to the NGOs. India has been experimenting since 1960s with flexible systems giving freedom to the NGOs to set up SHGs. Even some NGOs have developed innovative and people-centred approach in the identification of the poor, formation and development of SHGs in microfinance under NABARD's programme. The functioning methodology of NGOs, in many cases, is project based and they are engaged with the time-bound programmes. Banks have been apathetic to SHGs linkage partly because the concept has yet to percolate to the branch level with each bank having its own guidelines. Also SHG lending is not perceived as normal lending activity, but treated as a concessional dispensation. My personal encounter with the group members and staff of the MRYDO unveils the fact that there is a greater demand for the banks to provide the loan. There are many successful examples of microcredit programmes in rural India, but few have had a specific focus on urban India. The experiences of NGOs like MRYDO that is operating over a decade show that the poor are bankable. It illustrates that microcredit can be used as a core instrument of empowerment for the urban poor. Emancipation of women is an essential pre-requisite for economic development and social progress of the nation. One of the major contributions of microfinance is towards women's empowerment.

NOTES AND REFERENCES

1. "Gender refers to the social construction of relations between men and women. Our concern is to ensure that difference is not used to discriminate against any group or individual. The state and society need to eradicate all forms of subordination, oppression and discrimination based on gender" (Dasharathi, 2008: 42).
2. World Bank (2005): *World Development Report*. Washington D.C.: Oxford University Press, p. 8.
3. P. Tarafdar (2008): 'Policies and Programmes for Women's Empowerment in the South Asian Context' In: *New Dimensions of Women Empowerment* (ed.) A.K. Sinha. New Delhi: Deep and Deep Publications Pvt. Ltd., p. 26.
4. S. Bharadwaj-Badal (2009): *Gender, Social Structure and Empowerment: Status Report of Women in India*. Jaipur: Rawat Publications, pp. 147-48.
5. D. Padmavathi (2008): 'Empowerment of Women through Microfinance'. In: *Empowerment in India: Vision for 21st Century* (ed.) R. Pandya. New Delhi: New Century Publications, p. 331.
6. *Ibid*. p. 336.
7. R.K. Siwach (2004): *Voluntary Organisations and Social Welfare*. Delhi: Shankar Publications, pp. 3-4.
8. D.L. Sills (1968): 'Voluntary Association: Sociological Aspects'. *International Encyclopaedia of Social Sciences*, New York: The Macmillan Company & The Free Press, Vol.16, pp. 362-63.
9. Government of India (1992): 'Sectoral Programmes of Development'. *Eighth Five Year Plan 1992-97*, Vol. II. New Delhi: Planning Commission, p. 39.
10. K. Mustafa, Z.A. Gill and T. Azid (2000): 'NGOs, Microfinance and Poverty Alleviation: Experience of the Rural Poor in Pakistan'. *The Pakistan Development Review*, Vol. 39, No. 4, Part II, pp. 771-72.
11. H.K. Anheier and L.M. Salamon (1998): *The Non-profit Sector in the Developing World: A Comparative Analysis*, Manchester: Manchester University Press, pp. 2-3.
12. D. Rajasekhar and R.R. Biradar (2004): *Reluctant Partners Coming*

Together? Interface between People, Government and the NGOs, New Delhi: Concept Publishing Company, pp. xiii-xiv.
13. S.N. Biswas and U. Aggarwal (2005): 'Human Resource Needs of Rural Development NGOs in India'. *Working Paper 187*. Gujurat: Institute of Rural Management Anand, pp. 2-3.
14. S. Shigetomi (2002): 'The State and NGOs: Issues and Analytical Framework'. In: *The State and NGOs: Perspective from Asia*. S. Shigetomi (ed.). Singapore: Institute of Southeast Asian Studies, pp. 6-7.
15. N. Bava (1997): Introduction. In: *Non-Governmental Organisations in Development: Theory and Practice*, New Delhi: Kanishka Publishers, p. 6.
16. *Ibid*. p. 6.
17. C.K. Gariyali and S.K. Vettivel (2006): *Pillars of Hope: NGOs in Women Self-Help Movement of Tamil Nadu*. New Delhi: Vetri Publishers, p. 3.
18. *Ibid*. p. 4.
19. Government of India (1992): p. 35.
20. Government of India (2002): 'Sectoral Policies and Programmes'. *Tenth Five Year Plan 2002-07*, Vol. II. New Delhi: Planning Commission, p. 306.
21. A 'shadow state' refers to a parastatal apparatus consisting of voluntary organisations charged with the responsibility of providing services, which otherwise, would have been provided by the state (Rajasekhar and Biradar, 2004: 32). The term was coined by Wolch (1990).
22. S. Sen (1999): Some Aspects of State NGO Relationships in India in the Post-Independence Era. *Development and Change*, Vol. 30, No. 2, pp. 327-55.
23. D. Rajasekhar and R.R. Biradar (2004): pp. xiv.
24. Government of India (1992): p. 39.
25. D. Rajasekhar and R.R. Biradar (2004): pp. xvii-xviii.
26. J. Pearce (2005): 'Development, NGOs and Civil Society: The Debate and its Future'. In: *Development, NGOs and Civil Society*. Jaipur: Rawat Publications, p. 29.
27. S.N. Biswas and U. Aggarwal (2005): p. 1.
28. S. Dharmarajan (1998): *NGO Development Initiative and Public Policy*. New Delhi: Kaniska Publishers, Distributors, pp. 12-13.
29. D.C. Korten (1990): *Getting to the 21st Century: Voluntary Action and the Global Agenda*. West Hartford: Kumarian Press, p. 100.
30. S. Shigetomi (2002): p. 11.
31. *Ibid*. p. 11.
32. *Ibid*. p. 12.
33. *Ibid*. p. 17.
34. Government of India (2002): p. 275.

35. D. Rajasekhar and R.R. Biradar (2004): p. 20.
36. *Ibid.* pp. 22-23.
37. National Bank for Agriculture and Rural Development (1999): *'Gender Equality: Empowerment of Rural Women through NABARD Schemes'*, Mumbai: NABARD, p. 14.
38. K.G. Karmakar (1999): *Rural Credit and Self-Help Groups: Microfinance Needs and Concepts in India.* New Delhi: Sage Publications, pp. 168-169.
39. *Ibid.* p. 170.
40. *Ibid.* p. 171.
41. *Ibid.* p. 211.
42. *Ibid.* p. 292.
43. D. Rajasekhar, N.K. Gowda and R. Manjula (2006): *Impact of Bank Interest rates on SHG Members*, New Delhi: Concept Publishing Company, p. 25.
44. P. Satish (2005): 'Mainstreaming of Indian Microfinance', *Economic and Political Weekly*, Vol. XL, No. 17, p. 1734.
45. S. Roy Choudhury (2003): 'Old Classes and New Spaces: Urban Poverty, Unorganised Labour and New Unions', *Economic and Political Weekly*, Vol. XXXVIII, No. 50, p. 5278.
46. K.G. Karmakar (1999): p. 294.
47. *Ibid.* p. 295.
48. K. Anand (2008): 'I-banks lose Flavour, IIM Students eye Micro-fin', *The Economic Times*, New Delhi, (24 Sept.), p. 7.
49. K.G. Karmakar (1999): p. 298.
50. *Ibid.* p. 299.
51. *http://www.indiatogether.org/2003/oct/pov-credscene.htm*
52. R. Dasgupta (2001): 'An Informal Journey through Self-Help Groups', *Indian Journal of Agricultural Economics*, Vol. 56, No. 3, pp. 370-86.
53. S.N. Tilekar, N.J. Naikade, B.J. Deshmukh and A.A. Patil (2001): 'Women Self-Help Groups Affiliated to 'Chaitanya': A Study on Pune District', *Indian Journal of Agricultural Economics*, Vol. 56, No. 3, p. 458.
54. Government of India (2002): p. 275.
55. V. Puhazhendi and K.J.S. Satyasayi (2001): 'Econojmic and Social Empowerment of Rural Poor through Self-Help Groups', *Indian Journal of Agricultural Economics*, Vol. 56, No. 3, p. 451.
56. S. Lakshmanan (2001): 'Working of Self-Help Groups with Particular Reference to Mallipalayam Self-Help Group, Gobichettipalayam Block, Erode District, Tamil Nadu', *Indian Journal of Agricultural Economics*, Vol. 56, No. 3, p. 457.

57. N.V. Namboodiri and R.L. Shiyani (2001): 'Potential Role of Self-Help Groups in Rural Financial Deepening', *Indian Journal of Agricultural Economics*, Vol. 56, No. 3, p. 408.
58. C.L. Dadhich (2001): 'Microfinance—A Panacea for Poverty Alleviation: A Case of Oriental Grameen Project in India', *Indian Journal of Agricultural Economics*, Vol. 56, No. 3, p. 421.
59. S.N. Tilekar, *et al.* (2001): p. 458.
60. K. Vatta (2003): 'Microfinance and Poverty Alleviation', *Economic and Political Weekly*, Vol. XXXVIII, No. 5, p. 433.
61. *http://www.indiatogether.org/2003/oct/pov-credscene.htm*

Conclusion and Suggestions

Microfinance is the provision of financial services to the poor who are otherwise deemed unfit by the conventional banking network. Microfinance is the provision of a broad range of financial services such as deposits, loans, payment services, money transfers and insurance to poor and low income households and their microenterprises. Definitions of microfinance differ from country to country. Some of the criteria of microfinance which are generally being used include: (i) the loans are micro or very small in size; (ii) the target users are micro-entrepreneurs and low-income households; (iii) funds are utilised for income generation, enterprise development and social purposes like health, education, marriage, etc.; and (iv) most terms and conditions for microfinance loans are flexible and easy to understand and are suited to the local conditions of the community.

Microfinance has grown rapidly since the late 1990s due to the following reasons. The reasons are: (i) ability to reach out to the poor; (ii) promise of financial sustainability; (iii) the potential to build on traditional systems; (iv) provision of informal and flexible financial services to the poor for meeting their modest consumption and livelihood needs; (v) the availability of better financial products as result of experimentation and innovation; and (vi) provision for collateral-free microcredit to the poor.

There are two ways of looking at the Indian society; one is rural and the other one is urban. The underdeveloped rural areas remain one of the prime aspects of concern. The rural areas are not able to accommodate the demand of the labour folk. As a result, the push-pull factor is the reason for which the imbalance is created. The unstoppable migration of people from rural to urban areas creates havoc, leading to mushrooming of slums, congestions, diseases, crimes, etc. The central dogma is urban poverty. Therefore, withdrawing attention from this aspect of development and ignoring the urban poor from their development would seriously harm the social opportunities, and thus creating an imbalance therein. Therefore, the space is now created for these stateless urban people to think of microfinance, which can bring a bit of relief in the management of their life and family.

The urban poor are heterogeneous in composition. The place of origin, caste, religion, language and the overall background of socialisation are some of the elements that make the urban poor too much heterogeneous. The occupations that they carry out in urban locations also differ from what they ought have done at the place of their origin. The social connection as such becomes a vacuum for them. The day and night become a passing time for them, as the target is to fill up their empty vessel. There is no room for them to think of savings and credit. Even if they think of any credit, is there any financial institution ready to provide them? At this position introducing microfinance for the stateless urban poor probably help at surpassing the critical juncture of life.

It is estimated that the country will have more than 40 per cent of its population in urban areas by the year 2030. While the number of rural poor decreased from 25.7 crores (257 million) to 19.3 crores (193 million) between 1991 and 2001, the number of urban poor actually increased from 5.2 crores (52 million) to 6.7 crores (67 million). Despite the large number of urban poor, most of them have little or no access to formal financial services. There is relatively little outreach of microfinance in major urban areas today.

There are three basic problems regarding the study of Urban Microfinance. *Firstly,* there are no clear estimates of the number of people in urban areas with any access to organised financial services. This may be attributed to the migratory nature of the urban poor, comprising mostly of migrants from rural areas. Even moneylenders often shy away from lending to urban poor. *Secondly,* there have been a few instances of MFIs venturing into this area of lending to urban poor that are undertaking micro-enterprises and small business activities. Urban branches of banks, even though having manpower and technology support, are not attuned to SHG lending or microfinance. *Thirdly,* at present, NABARD is permitted, as per its Act and Mandate, to support microfinance activities in rural and semi-urban areas only. An enabling provision has to be made in the NABARD Act, 1981 permitting the NABARD to provide microfinance services to the urban poor.

The urbanisation process of Delhi has a chequered history. In the 2001 Census, Delhi occupies the first place with 93.01 per cent people living in urban areas. It is also evident that the dynamics and challenges in the urban environment vis-à-vis microfinance are unique and distinct from rural areas. Thus, providing urban microfinancial services can be a tremendous opportunity, given the gravity of the prevailing situation, existing demand and expanding market. A large influx of people from distress rural India have moved to urban centres for better opportunities and used Delhi as a shelter zone in the form of slums, the old villages and Peripheral Villages.

There are different approaches through which the microfinance can be understood better. Among these, the group approach is familiar in India. Savings, loans, and loan repayments are taken care of at the group level. The group, basically, is known as Self-Help Group (SHG). The SHGs are small, informal and homogeneous groups of not more than 20 members. The homogeneous nature of the group ensures that the members do not have conflicting interests and can participate freely. The members have poor risk-taking ability, no collateral to offer and have limited earning opportunities.

In the programmes related to group lending, the functions of screening, monitoring and enforcement of repayment, to a large extent, are transferred from the bank's agent to the borrowers, that is, the group members themselves. Group members can perform all such functions more effectively and at a relatively lower cost. Thus, the transaction costs are reduced. The group uses the money according to its requirement among the members. Therefore, the mismatch between demand and supply is minimised. In addition to this, there is also some flexibility of loan repayment.

The advantages of the SHG can be seen from economic, social, environmental and technological point of view. SHG works as an economic unit. It is like a bank with an aim to savings, credits and returns for the members. SHG is a homogeneous social unit. It is not only a platform to interact among members but also a place of sharing happiness, sorrow, misery, misfortune, etc. and a way to get rid of the unwanted. The members do exchange ideas about the indigenous knowledge basically relating to the craft mechanism. Therefore, the group is a unit reservoir of socio-cultural capital. The group sometimes contributes time and strength for the welfare of neighbours and community. They often resolve conflicts and mistrust of theirs and others.

The SHG-Bank Linkage Programme was launched by NABARD as a pilot project in February 1992. There are certain objectives of the linkage programme such as (a) to evolve supplementary strategy for meeting the credit needs of the poor by combining informal sector credit system with formal credit institutions, (b) to build up mutual trust and confidence between the banker and the rural poor, (c) to encourage banking activity, and (d) to improve flow of credit to rural poor with reduced transaction cost, both for the financing bank and the borrower.

There are certain issues on extending the SHG-Bank Linkage Scheme to urban areas. The issues are such as the following: (i) There are no clear estimates of the number of poor people in urban areas and their no accessibility to organised financial services. (ii) Urban branches of banks, even though having manpower and technology support, are not attuned to SHG lending or microfinance. (iii) The multiple and diversified activities of the banks act as barrier to cater to the microfinance market segment. In 2008, the Committee on Financial Inclusion has recommended amendment to

NABARD Act to enable it to provide microfinance services to the urban poor.

Delhi is located at 28°37'N to 28°61'N and 77°14'E to 77°23'E. It borders the Indian States of Uttar Pradesh on East and Haryana on West, North and South. Located on the banks of river Yamuna in northern India, Delhi emerged as a major political, cultural and commercial city along the trade routes between northwest India and the Indo-Gangetic plains. Owing to the immigration of people from across the country, Delhi has grown to be a cosmopolitan city. Its rapid development and urbanisation, coupled with the relatively high average income of its population, has transformed the city. Today, Delhi is a major cultural, political, and commercial centre of India.

There are three local bodies (statutory towns) viz., New Delhi Municipal Council (42.7 sq.km), Delhi Cantonment Board (43 sq.km) and Delhi Municipal Corporation (1,397.3 sq.km). According to the Census of India 2001, the population of Delhi was 13.85 million, which included 7.61 million males and 6.24 million females. Pronounced urban characteristics of the population could be seen by the fact that 93.6 per cent population of Delhi had been residing in urban areas. The corresponding population density was 9,340 persons per sq. km. There are nine districts and 27 tehsils out of which 16 tehsils in Delhi have rural areas.

The transformation of urban morphology of Delhi has to be understood through the process of peopling in relation to the social composition of the residing population. The peopling process is subject to a series of events over time and space. There is a direct relationship between the peopling process and the events that guided Delhi to its present form. In Delhi, there were as many as 300 villages according to the Census of 1961. It is now with 165 villages out of which there are 158 inhabited villages according to the Census of India, 2001. Apart from these, there are unauthorised colonies.

The concepts of Enclave and Peripheral Villages are very much subjective. The Enclave Villages provide urban characteristics as they are surrounded completely by the urban elements and amenities. On the contrary, the Peripheral Villages are of rural in nature. Yet, these villages provide some elements of urbanism, as there is a continuous interaction between the Peripheral Villages with the urban centres of Delhi.

The research methodology has been adopted for assessing the impact of microfinance as a tool for understanding the life of people in Delhi. The research methodology includes the objectives, the selection of the study area, data collection process, building and testing of interview schedule, sample size and implementation of sampling techniques and the statistical tools employed to analyses and present the data.

The objectives of the present study are: (i) to analyse the pattern of socio-demographic and educational status of the SHG members, (ii) to investigate the economic profile of the SHG members, (iii) to evaluate the impact assessment of microfinance through credit and asset structure, (iv) to measure the role of NGOs for implementation of microfinance, and (v) to augment the strategy for better implementation of microfinance.

Primary data have been collected by way of floating interview schedule to collect the information from the respondents who are the members of SHGs in the Enclave and Peripheral Villages in the areas of Delhi. The survey was conducted between the months of September and November 2008 by visiting the SHG members with the NGO staff and local people. The area of the present study belongs primarily, to the South-West District, West District and North-West District of Delhi. The women members of SHGs interviewed by the researcher belong to 22 villages.

A three-tier system has been employed to collect data: firstly, the selection of villages and colonies; secondly, the selection of SHGs; and thirdly, selection of focus group members. The sampling techniques adopted in this context are the judgement sampling, the convenience sampling and the snowball sampling to follow up the above three stages respectively. Altogether 110 SHGs (91 per cent) were consulted out of the total 121 existing SHGs, which included 52 SHGs (88 per cent) and 58 SHGs (94 per cent) from the Enclave Villages and Peripheral Villages respectively. Altogether, 219 group members with 104 and 115 women members from the Enclave Villages and Peripheral Villages were interviewed respectively.

In the sample, there are maximum members in the category of age group of 31-40 years. It is 36.54 per cent and 42.61 per cent in the Enclave and Peripheral Villages respectively. The average age of the sample group members is 37.79 years. The average age of sample group members is 35.9 and 39.5 years in the Enclave and Peripheral Villages respectively. The average number of children per the group member stands at 2.73, which includes 2.69 and 2.76 in the Enclave and Peripheral Villages respectively. However, the average household size for the sample group members is 4.9 with 4.91 and 4.89 in the Enclave and Peripheral Villages respectively. This relates to the fact that there is no much variation between these two types of settlements.

Altogether, 90 per cent of group members are married. It is 92.17 per cent for the members in the Peripheral Villages and 87.5 per cent in the Enclave Villages. There is higher percentage of illiterates in the sample groups of Peripheral Villages (34.78) than in the Enclave Villages (21.15). The group members at the level of matriculation are 27.88 per cent and 29.57 per cent in case of Enclave and Peripheral Villages respectively.

In the Enclave Villages, 76.92 per cent of group members belong to nuclear families, and only 23.08 per cent of members belong to joint families. In the Peripheral Villages, the pattern is not different. It is 75.65 per cent and 24.35 per cent towards nuclear and joint families respectively. All the group members in the Peripheral Villages have *pacca* (cemented) houses. In the Enclave Villages, 98 per cent group members have *pacca* houses leaving a few who dwells in the *kachha* houses (only 2 per cent). There are 90.38 per cent of group members who have own residences and 9.62 per cent of members staying on rented accommodation in the Enclave Villages. Whereas, 99.13 per cent of group members have own residences in the Peripheral Villages.

Regarding the place of birth of SHG members in the Enclave settlement, it is found that almost 49.04 per cent of sample SHG members were born in Delhi, while 50.96 per cent of members were born outside Delhi. In the Peripheral Villages, 68.7 per cent of SHG members were born outside Delhi and 31.3 per cent of members were born in Delhi. In Enclave Villages, it is found that 86.79 per cent of members out of the total members born outside of Delhi have migrated to the city along with their husbands. In the Peripheral Villages, almost 96.20 per cent members out of the total members born outside Delhi had self-migration induced by marriage.

It is found that over the years between 2000 and 2008, there is a rising trend among the members to join the SHGs. A little less than 5 per cent of sample members had joined the SHGs till 2000. The significant rise was observed in the subsequent years. It was 21.74 per cent in 2003 and 2004, which rose to 33.91 per cent in 2005 and 2006, though, it came a bit down to 33.04 per cent in 2007 and 2008.

Regarding the sources that motivate the people to join SHGs, it is found that little over 4 per cent of people are influenced by the family to join SHGs, followed by 41.55 per cent through neighbours, friends and relatives and 54.34 per cent by the NGOs. Furthermore, it is found that 82.19 per cent of sample members belong to the SHGs whose size comprises of 20 members followed by 19 members (9.59 per cent), and 18 and less members (8.22 per cent).

In the sample study it is found that a large section of the SHG members are homemakers (62.10 per cent) followed by those involved in professional work, shopkeeping and dairy business (22.37 per cent), service holders (8.68 per cent), unskilled and skilled labourers (4.57 per cent) and students (2.28 per cent). In Enclave Villages, it is found that a larger number of SHG members spend their time as homemakers (65.38 per cent). Second to this category, 13.46 per cent of members are engaged in services. There are students (4.81 per cent) as well. The picture on occupation in the Peripheral Villages is slightly different, where 59.13 per cent of SHG members spend their time as homemakers followed by professional work, shop keeping and dairy business (33.91 per cent).

A major chunk of members (44.29 per cent) lie in the income category of Rs. 30,001-Rs. 60,000, which includes 51.92 per cent and 37.39 per cent in the Enclave and Peripheral Villages respectively. It is understood that the average annual income (AAI) per SHG member household from all sources is Rs. 71,326. This includes Rs. 68,054 and Rs. 74,285 for the Enclave Villages and Peripheral Villages respectively. The average annual expenditure (AAE) of the sample households in this study stands at Rs. 60,798. This includes Rs. 56,213 and Rs. 64,864 per household in the Enclave and Peripheral Villages respectively. The annual surplus per household in the sample is Rs. 10,528 which includes Rs. 11,841 and Rs. 9,421 in the Enclave and Peripheral Villages respectively.

In the Enclave Villages, the distance indices vary between 0.28 and 1.67. The mean standard deviation is 0.50 with coefficient of variation 50 per cent. In the Peripheral Villages, the distance indices vary between 0.63 and 1.42. The mean standard deviation is 0.26 with coefficient of variation 26 per cent. In the villages taken together, the distance indices vary between 0.23 and 1.65. The mean standard deviation is 0.39 with coefficient of variation 39 per cent. It is observed that the villages nearer to the destinations show lower index than the farther villages. The villages with very low index are in complete advantageous position.

Out of the 80.37 per cent of sample members who have availed the credit, 82.69 per cent and 78.26 per cent belong to the Enclave and Peripheral Villages respectively. Among the members who have availed credit from different sources, only a thin per cent of members (1.70) has been found to have borrowed from relatives and friends, followed by 5.68 per cent of members who have availed credit from single source, i.e., bank. However a large section of members (65.34 per cent) have availed credit from intra-group funds. Almost 27.27 per cent of members have availed credit from double sources, such as SHGs and banks.

In the present sample study on SHG members, 31.82 per cent of members are found to have availed credit for more than one purpose, which includes 23.26 per cent and 40 per cent in the Enclave and Peripheral Villages respectively. Of the 22.17 per cent of members who availed credits for social purposes, they are as high as 27.91 per cent in the Enclave Villages and as low as 16.66 per cent in Peripheral Villages.

The study shows that the average annual return per group is Rs. 5,774. It is Rs. 5,461 in the Enclave settlement and Rs. 6,008 in the Peripheral settlement. Whereas, the average annual returns per member is Rs. 269, which includes Rs. 282 and Rs. 306 in the Enclave and Peripheral Villages respectively.

Out of the 94.06 per cent of households of SHG members who possess assets, Enclave Villages have 92.31 per cent and 95.65 per cent belong to the Peripheral Villages. A thin percentage of members (5.94) does not have assets in their house. This constitutes 7.69 per cent and 4.35 per cent in the Enclave and Peripheral Villages respectively. Out of the asset typology, cattleheads have been bought by 28.95 per cent of member households. Cattleheads are found with the households belonging to the Peripheral Villages (44.68 per cent). In addition, 26.32 per cent of members have accumulated more than one asset that includes 24.14 per cent and 27.66 per cent members in the Enclave and Peripheral Villages respectively.

There are 91.32 per cent of members satisfied with the working and functioning of the SHGs as against 8.68 per cent of members who are found not satisfied. It is 90.38 per cent and 92.17 per cent in the Enclave and Peripheral Villages respectively. A few sample members (8.68 per cent) are not satisfied with the functioning of SHGs, who constitute 9.62 per cent and 7.83 per cent in the Enclave and Peripheral Villages respectively. There are 41 per cent, 42.5 per cent and 16.5 per cent of satisfied members who express their view on SHGs as good, very good and excellent respectively.

For empowerment of women, initiatives have been made by the women's movement. A widespread network of NGOs has strong grassroots presence and deep insight into women's concerns. Microfinance programmes have the potential to transform power relations and empower the poor—both men and women. In its simplest form, an NGO is a body of people who come together to provide help to those who fail to accumulate sufficient resources to survive.

In its most ambitious form, an NGO is a private, not-for-profit institution dedicated to influencing the working structure of government and ensure the greater welfare of all citizens. There is no universal classification system of NGOs. They could be grouped on their relationship with the state, operating philosophy, advocacy issues, target groups, etc. United Nations (UN) clearly specifies that an NGO must be independent from the direct control of any government. There are a few key characteristics of NGOs. An NGO is (i) independent of government control, (ii) a private organisation, (iii) not constituted as a political party, (iv) a non-profit-making organisation, (v) essentially non-violent, and (vi) broadly geared towards improving/changing the existing conditions of the society.

The state in developing countries like India has the greatest responsibility to bring about planned socio-economic development and nation building. The state is not an end in itself but a means to an end and that end is to promote all-round, balanced, integrated development of all citizens and the nation as a whole. The civil society manifests itself through myriads of households, communities, associations, voluntary groups of different hues and kinds, social service workers, non-profit organizations, cooperatives, unions, women's development groups and environmental NGOs. Not only does it have its definite place in modern state but also performs vital functions for its members through the network of these institutions.

Despite NGO weaknesses such as spatial limitations, allegation on their accountability and constraints in working at micro levels, they have been gaining importance in service delivery and have become a prominent member of civil society. This has resulted in the proliferation of NGOs, diversification and multiplication of their activities and rapid flow of resources from government and donors.

The Government Officials perceive poverty to be the inability to access basic needs due to low income. In contrast, the NGOs have wider perception of poverty, which includes vulnerability, powerlessness, isolation and assetlessness. NGOs emphasize on building of the organisations of the poor through process-oriented approach and strengthen their institutional capacity to address the root cause of poverty. During past few decades that NGOs are becoming increasingly important in the people-oriented development programmes and projects at the grassroots level by virtue their involvement and commitment to the rural poor.

India has been experimenting since 1960s with flexible systems, giving a lot of freedom to the NGOs to set up SHGs. A pilot project for linking SHGs with banks was introduced in 1992 by NABARD to encourage thrift and savings among the rural poor and to supplement their credit needs through the banking system.

SHGs set up by NGOs, with the assistance of bank linkage, ensure individual loans for women beneficiaries and individual/joint liability for repayment. The stress is less on asset creation and more on production-*cum*-consumption loans, ensuring quicker repayment and less borrower fatigue in loan repayment. The repayment rate is much higher in SHGs as there is no subsidy involved.

Banks have been apathetic to SHG-linkage partly because the concept has yet to percolate to the branch level with each bank having its own guidelines. Also SHG lending is not perceived as normal lending activity, but treated as a concessional dispensation. Most bankers distrust lending to the poor and to NGOs due to the poor credibility of existing poverty alleviation programmes and poor interaction between NGOs and banks. On their part, NGOs also distrust banks and their bureaucratic procedures.

NGOs around the world have led the campaign to expand banking services to the poor. There are many successful examples of microcredit programmes in rural India, but few have had a specific focus on urban India. The NGO's experiences like that of MRYDO show that the poor are bankable. It illustrates that microcredit can be used as a core instrument of empowerment for the urban poor. When used in conjunction with other programmes, it actually serves to improve the quality of life of the urban poor. Till now the MRYDO has been able to promote 256 SHGs covering 5120 women in different locations in Delhi. More than 150 SHGs have been linked with SBI, CBI and Allahabad Bank availing loan worth more than Rs. 175 lakhs, and repayment is 100 per cent.

The country-wide network of more than 12,000 Voluntary Organisations have been playing a very significant role in the empowerment of women and development of children as they share the major burden of implementing Governmental policies and programmes. Their initiatives have often proved to be successful alternatives in the areas of women's literacy, support services, microcredit for poor women, employment and income generation, gender sensitisation, organising women into SHGs and fight against atrocities on women and the girl child, etc.

The impact of SHGs has relatively been more pronounced on social aspects than on the economic aspects. Emancipation of women is an essential prerequisite for economic development and social progress of the nation. One of the major contributions of microfinance is towards women's empowerment. It is revealed that SHGs are really a boon in the rural and urban areas, which give women financial autonomy and make them economically independent. As women's groups exclusively dominate the SHGs, their empowerment both on the economic and social fronts is one of the greatest opportunities in the mainstream of developmental activities.

Suggestions

After studying the SHGs in the urban context, the following suggestions have been aired, as given below:

- There should be integrated developmental activities throughout the country filling the gap between rural-urban and regional disparities as regards all social indicators like poverty, education, employment and empowerment.

- Further augmenting steps are to be taken in minimising the rural-urban migration.
- The NABARD should enhance its scope for the urban areas on the issues of microfinance.
- The SHG-Bank linkage should be enhanced, so that the timely credit requirement for the group is realised.
- Intermediation of NGOs should be encouraged by the funding agencies for opportunity/employment development. As far as the formation of SHGs is concerned, NGOs should focus more on the needy individuals.
- Monitoring, supervision and timely audit should be conducted by the funding agencies in order to assess the activities carried out by the NGOs towards the improvement of the SHGs.
- Steps should be taken for the proper market linkage for the products manufactured by SHGs, especially the embroidery works done by the women in the study area.
- Encouraging the participation by more number of banks through the public-private partnership may shorten the delay for the grant of credit to the SHGs.

Appendix 1

AN INTERVIEW SCHEDULE FOR COLLECTION OF DATA FROM THE URBAN POOR FOR STUDY ON MICROFINANCE

By: Dr. Chittaranjan Dash, PGDBM (FM) 2007-08, National Institute of Financial Management (Ministry of Finance, GoI), Pali Road, Sector-48, Faridabad, Haryana. Tel: 9999494239.

Date of Data Collection: ....

I. General Information

1. Name: ....
2. Father/Husband's Name: ....
3. Sex: Male/Female
4. Age .... (Yr.)
5. Name of the Head of your Family ....
6. What is the relation of Head with the Respondent? ......
   ....
7. House No. : ....
8. Village/Colony: ....
9. P.S.: ....
10. District: ....
11. State: ....
12. Telephone (if any): ....

II. Demographic Information

1. Are you Unmarried/Married/Divorcee/Widow(er)?
2. Age at marriage .... (year).
3. Have you got any Child? (Yes / No)
4. If yes, How many? .... (Son .... Daughter ....) Total Adults
5. Are you Illiterate/literate? If literate, state your Educational Status? ....
6. State your occupation? (House Wife/Unskilled Labour/ Skilled Labour/Business/Service/Any other) ....
7. State the occupation of your Husband/Wife? (House Wife/Unskilled Labour/Skilled Labour/Business/ Service/Any other) ....
8. State the Source of your income? ....
9. What is your Approximate Annual Income? .... (Rs.)
10. Type of your family? (Nuclear/Joint)
11. Type of House? (*Kachha/Pacca*)
12. Whether this house is your Own or on Rent? (Own/ Rent)
13. Total No. of Family Members staying together? (Male: Female:)
14. Since how many years you have been staying in this city?
15. Can you mention place of your origin?
16. Who migrated to this city? (Yourself/Husband/ Parents/ Grandparents/Any Other..................)

III. Self-Help Group (SHG) Information

1. Are you currently a member of any SHG? (Yes/No)
2. If yes, since when? (Year of joining ....), SHG No.:................, SHG Name
3. Who motivated you to join the SHG? (Family Member/ Friend/Relative/Government/NGO/Cooperative Society/Others............)
4. What is the nature of your SHG? (Grameen Mode/ Govt. System/Cooperative/Any Other.................)

5. How many members are there in your SHG?
6. What is your monthly average expenses for running your SHG?.................(Rs.)
7. What is your total annual return from your SHG?................(Rs.)
8. How do you distribute your income among the members? ....
9. What amount do you save per month?......................(Rs.)
10. Why this much amount and not more? ....
11. Have you ever availed any loan? (Yes/No)
12. From where you have borrowed? (Relative/Friend/ SHG Members/Banks/Pvt. Money Lender/ Others................)
13. If from the Bank, Name the Bank................
14. Under what rate of interest?................
15. What is the loan amount?.................(Rs.)
16. Duration of the loan?................
17. State the purpose of loan?................
18. What are the hurdles you face for approving the loan amount?................
19. Are you paying back the instalment? (Yes/No)
20. If no, Why?................
21. What is the amount of your instalment? ....(Rs.)
22. Do you get support from your husband/wife/any family member (Relation: ....) in paying back the instalment? (Yes/No)

IV. Annual Average Expenditure Pattern of SHG Member

1. What are your main areas of expenditure? ....
2. Expenditure on Children Education: (Rs.) ....
3. Expenditure on Health: (Rs.) ....
4. Expenditure on Loan Repayment: (Rs.) ....
5. Expenditure on Livelihood: (Rs.) ....
6. Paying to the Husband's Requirement: (Rs.) ....
7. Expenditure on Children and Self Clothing: (Rs.) ....
8. Expenditure on House Rent: (Rs.) ....

9. Expenditure on Utensils: (Rs.) ....
10. Expenditure on Consumer Durables: (Rs.) ....
11. Expenditure on Gift and Social Obligations: (Rs.)................
12. Expenditure on Conveyance: (Rs.) ....
13. Other Expenditure: (Rs.) ....

V. Role of NGOs in the Development of SHGs

1. Is there any NGO, which is helping your SHG? (Yes/No)
2. If yes, Name the NGO?................
3. Where this NGO is situated? ....
4. What type of support you are getting from this NGO? (Social / Technical / Financial / Business / Any Other................)
5. If Financial, what amount you are getting and on what basis? (Rs)................(With Rate of Interest lesser than that of Market Rate of Interest/Only Principal with Limited Time Period/Other................)
6. If Technical, What type of Support? (Capital/Technology / Training / Management / Any Other................)
7. If you avail these Technical Supports from the Market, the expected cost incurred (Rs.)................
8. Do you get Social Support in terms of Place/Building/Social Security/Any Other................
9. Do you deal the NGOs for Business Purpose? (Yes/No)
10. If Yes, for Getting Raw Material/Selling Intermediate or Finished Products.
11. Do you get Proper Price for your value added products from the NGOs? (Yes/No)
12. If Yes, Equivalent to Govt. Declaration/Market Conditions/NGOs' Policy/Other.
13. Does the NGO help in finalising the loan from the Micro-financer? (Yes/No)

VI. Impact of Joining SHG

1. Does your family have any household assets like TV, Refrigerator, etc.? (Yes/No)
2. Have these (household assets) been purchased after you join the SHG? (Yes/No)
3. What are the household assets that you have in your house? (Yes/No)

Household Assets	*Before Joining SHG*	*After Joining SHG*
(a) Land		
(b) House		
(c) Motor Cycle		
(d) Four Wheeler		
(e) Watch (Wall & Wrist)		
(f) Television		
(g) Refrigerator		
(h) Fan		
(i) Tractor		
(j) Telephone		
(k) Camera		
(l) Music System		
(m) Animals (Cow/Bull/Buffalo/Mule/Donkey/Horse)		
(n) Cart (Bull/Horse/Mule/Buffalo/Donkey)		
(o) Rickshaw		
(p) Any Other		

VII. Satisfaction of Running SHG:

1. Are you satisfied in running the SHG? (Yes/No)
2. If No, What are the causes of dissatisfaction?

   ....
3. If Yes, Rank your SHG (Excellent/Very Good/Good)

Appendix 2

Approximate Distance (in km) of Village/Colony from Important Destinations

Sl. No.	Village/ Colony	Type	District Head Quarter (HQ)		C.D.Block/Ward*		Police Station		Nearest Town		Bus Stop		Mandi		Local Hat	
			Name	Dis-tance	Name of HQ	Dis-tance	Name	Dis-tance	Name	Dis-tance	Name	Dis-tance	Name	Dis-tance	Name	Dis-tance
1.	Raghubir Block (Prem Nagar)	Enclave Village/ Colony	South-West Delhi (HQ: Kapas Hera)	12	Najafgarh	0.5	Najafgarh	0.5	Najafgarh	0.5	Najafgarh	0.5	Najafgarh	0.5	Najafgarh	0.5
2.	Roshan Garden	-do-	-do-	14	-do-	2	-do-	2	-do-	2	-do-	2	-do-	2	-do-	2
3.	Dharam Pura	-do-	-do-	13	-do-	1	-do-	1	-do-	1	-do-	1	-do-	1	-do-	1
4.	Surakhpur Road	-do-	-do-	16	-do-	4	-do-	4	-do-	4	-do-	4	-do-	4	-do-	4
5.	Roshan Pura	-do-	-do-	14	-do-	2	-do-	2	-do-	2	Chhawla Stand	1	-do-	2	-do-	2
6.	Shiv Enclave	-do-	-do-	17	-do-	3	-do-	3	-do-	3	Nangloi Stand	0.5	-do-	3	-do-	3

(Contd.)

(Contd.)

Sl. No.	Village/ Colony	Type	District Head Quarter (HQ)		C.D.Block/Ward*		Police Station		Nearest Town		Bus Stop		Mandi		Local Hat	
			Name	Distance	Name of HQ	Distance	Name	Distance	Name	Distance	Name	Distance	Name	Distance	Name	Distance
7.	Bijwasan	Enclave Village/ Colony	-do-	6	-do-	9	Kapas Hera	6	-do-	9	Bijwasan	0.5	-do-	9	-do-	9
8.	Nangli Sakrawati	-do-	-do-	16	-do-	4	Najafgarh	4	-do-	4	Sai Mandir Stand	2	-do-	3	-do-	3
9.	Kapas Hera	-do-	-do-	1	-do-	17	Kapas Hera	1	Najafgarh	17	Kapas Hera	1	-do-	17	Kapas Hera	1
10.	Laxmanpuri	-do-	West Delhi (HQ: Ram Pura)	14	Nangloi	15	Vikaspuri	10	-do-	5	Kakrola Mor Stand	0.5	-do-	4.5	-do-	4.5
11.	Mahabir Vihar	Peripheral Village/ Colony	North-West Delhi (HQ: Kanjhawala)	2	Ali Pur	10.5	Kanjhawala	2	Nangloi	12	Kanjhawala Chowk	1.5	Nangloi	12	Kanjhawala	2
12.	Dichaun	-do-	South-West Delhi (HQ: Kapas Hera)	18	Najafgarh	4	Najafgarh	4	Najafgarh	4	Najafgarh	4	Najafgarh	4	Najafgarh	4
13.	Surakh Pur	-do-	-do-	20	-do-	6	-do-	6	-do-	6	Surakhpur	0	-do-	6	-do-	6
14.	Jharoda	-do-	-do-	22	-do-	5	-do-	5	-do-	5	Jharoda	0	-do-	5	-do-	5
15.	Surera	-do-	-do-	23	-do-	6	Jaffarpur	5	-do-	6	Surera	0	-do-	6	-do-	6
16.	Pindwala Khurd	-do-	-do-	16	-do-	7	-do-	9	-do-	7	Pindwala Khurd	1	-do-	7	-do-	7
17.	Hasan Pur	-do-	-do-	20	-do-	10	-do-	13	-do-	10	Hasanpur Mor	1	-do-	10	-do-	10
18.	Rewla Kham Pur	-do-	-do-	15	-do-	5	Najafgarh	5	-do-	5	R. Kham Pur Mor	1	-do-	5	-do-	5

(Contd.)

(Contd.)

Sl. No.	Village/ Colony	Type	District Head Quarter (HQ)		C.D.Block/Ward*		Police Station		Nearest Town		Bus Stop		Mandi		Local Hat	
			Name	Dis-tance	Name of HQ	Dis-tance	Name	Dis-tance	Name	Dis-tance	Name	Dis-tance	Name	Dis-tance	Name	Dis-tance
19.	Kair	Peripheral village/ colony	-do-	22	-do-	7	Jaffarpur	8	-do-	7	Kair	0	-do-	7	-do-	7
20.	Baqar Garh	-do-	-do-	25	-do-	11	-do-	8	-do-	11	Baqargarh Mor	1.5	-do-	11	-do-	11
21.	Qazi Pur	-do-	-do-	30	-do-	12	-do-	10	-do-	12	Qazipur	0	-do-	12	-do-	12
22.	Khera Dabar	-do-	-do-	28	-do-	10	-do-	8	-do-	10	Khera Dabur	0	-do-	10	-do-	10

* In the area of National Capital Territory of Delhi, villages/colonies are administered by the New Delhi Municipal Council, Delhi Cantonment Board and Delhi Muncipal Corporation. Above these lies Delhi State Administration.

Bibliography

Anand, K. (2008): 'I-banks lose Flavour, IIM Students eye Micro-fin', *The Economic Times,* New Delhi (24 Sept.), p. 7.

Anheier, H.K. and L.M. Salamon (1998): *The Non-profit Sector in the Developing World: A Comparative Analysis.* Manchester: Manchester University Press.

Asian Development Bank (ADB) (2000): *Finance to the Poor: Microfinance Development Strategy,* Manila: ADB.

Basu, P. and P. Srivastava (2005): 'Exploring Possibilities: Microfinance and Rural Credit Access for the Poor in India', *Economic and Political Weekly,* Vol. XL, No. 17, pp. 1747-56.

Bava, N. (1997): Introduction. In: *Non-Governmental Organisations in Development: Theory and Practice,* New Delhi: Kanishka Publishers.

Bera, S. (2008): 'Programme Design and Impact Assessments: 'Success' of Microfinance in Perspective', *Economic and Political Weekly,* Vol. XLIII, No. 32, pp. 77-85.

Bharadwaj-Badal, S. (2009): *Gender, Social Structure and Empowerment: Status Report of Women in India,* Jaipur: Rawat Publications.

Biswas, S.N. and U. Aggarwal (2005): 'Human Resource Needs of Rural Development NGOs in India'. *Working Paper 187.* Gujurat: Institute of Rural Management Anand.

Blundell, R. and I. Preston (1996): 'Income, Expenditure and the Living Standards of UK Households', *Fiscal Studies,* Vol. 16, No. 3, pp. 40-54.

Bopegamage, A. (1957): *Delhi: A Study in Urban Sociology*, Bombay: University of Bombay.

Borbora, S. and R. Mahanta (2001): 'Micro Credit through Self-Help Groups and Its Impact: A Case of Rastriya Gramin Bank Vikas Nidhi Credit and Saving Programme in Assam', *Indian Journal of Agricultural Economics*, Vol. 56, No. 3, pp. 449-50.

Bouman, F.A.J. (1989): *'Small, Short and Unsecured: Informal Rural Finance in India'*, Delhi: Oxford University Press.

Breman, J. (2003): 'At the Bottom of the Urban Economy', *Economic and Political Weekly*, Vol. XXXVIII, No. 39, pp. 4151-58.

Brundtland, G.H. (1987): *Our Common Future: Brundtland Commission Report*, Delhi: Oxford University Press.

Bryman, A. (2008): *Social Research Methods*, Oxford: Oxford University Press.

Census of India (2001): *District Census Handbook, Series 8, Delhi*, Vol. 1

Census of India (2001): *India*, H Series.

Census of India (2001): *Primary Census Abstract*, Series 8, Delhi.

Census of India 2001: *Provisional Population Totals*, Series 8.

Census of India, 2001: *Provisional Population Totals* (Paper 2 of 2001 Rural-Urban Distribution of Population) Series 8, Delhi.

Choudhury, Md. S.H. (2000): 'On Sustainable Microfinance Operations', In. *Microfinance: Emerging Challenges* (eds.) K. Basu and K. Jindal, New Delhi: Tata McGraw-Hill Publishing Company Ltd.

Cohen, L. and M. Holliday (1982): *Statistics for Social Scientists*, London: Harper & Row.

Dadhich, C.L. (2001): 'Microfinance—A Panacea for Poverty Alleviation: A Case of Oriental Grameen Project in India', *Indian Journal of Agricultural Economics*, Vol. 56, No. 3, pp. 419-26.

Das, P. and P. Satish (2000): 'Microfinance—Present Scenario and Future Outlook', *BIRD's Eye View*, March, pp. 13-22.

Dasgupta, R. (2001): 'An Informal Journey through Self-Help Groups', *Indian Journal of Agricultural Economics,* Vol. 56, No. 3, pp. 370-86.

Dasgupta, R. (2005): 'Microfinance in India: Empirical Evidence, Alternative Models and Policy Imperatives'. *Economic and Political Weekly,* Vol. XL, No. 12, pp. 1229-37.

Dash, C. (2006): *Social Ecology and Demographic Structure: Narratives and Discourses,* New Delhi: Concept Publishing Company.

Dash, C. and B.S. Butola (2008): 'Understanding Bhotia Society and its Women Population through the Analytical Study of Proverbs—The Emblem of Oral Historiography', *Man in India,* Vol. 88, No. 4, pp. 653-64.

Dasharathi, Y.P. (2008): 'Gender Equity, Empowerment and Diversity'. In: *New Dimensions of Women Empowerment* (ed.) A.K. Sinha, New Delhi: Deep and Deep Publications Pvt. Ltd, pp. 40-54

Datta, S.K. and M. Raman (2001): 'Can Heterogeneity and Social Cohesion Coexist in Self-Help Groups?: An Evidence from Group Lending in Andhra Pradesh', *Indian Journal of Agricultural Economics,* Vol. 56, No. 3, pp. 387-418.

Dharmarajan, S. (1998): *NGO Development Initiative and Public Policy,* New Delhi: Kanishka Publishers and Distributors.

Dupont, V. (2000): 'Mobility Patterns and Economic Strategies of Houseless People in Old Delhi'. In: *Delhi: Urban Space and Human Destinies* (eds.) V. Dupont, E. Tarlo and D. Vidal, New Delhi: Manohar Publishers and Distributors, pp. 99-124.

Emeni, F.K. (2008): 'Micro Finance Institutions (MFIs) in Nigeria: Problems and Prospects: Questionnaire Survey Findings'. *Journal of Financial Management and Analysis,* Vol. 21, No. 1, pp. 69-76.

Fernandez, A.P. (2007): 'A Microfinance Institution with a Difference', *Economic and Political Weekly,* Vol. XLII, No. 13, pp. 1185-89.

Gariyali, C.K. and S.K. Vettivel (2006): *Pillars of Hope: NGOs* *in Women Self-Help Movement of Tamil Nadu,* New Delhi: Vetri Publishers.

Ghosh, J. (1994): 'The Expansionist City'. *Frontline,* Chennai, 20 May, p. 110.

Godelier, M. (1986): *The Mental and the Material: Thought Economy and Society,* England: Verso.

Goel, V. (2003): Delhi: *The Emperor's City,* New Delhi: Roli Books.

Goode, W. and P. Hatt (1952): *Methods in Social Research,* New York: McGraw Hill Book Company.

Gould, H.A. (2002): 'A Jajmani System of North India: Its Structure, Magnitude and Meaning'. In: *The Villages in India* (ed.) V. Madan, New Delhi: Oxford University Press, pp. 126-43.

Government of India (1992): 'Objectives, Perspectives, Macro-Dimensions, Policy Framework and Resources', *Eighth Five Year Plan 1992-97,* Vol. I, New Delhi: Planning Commission.

Government of India (1992): 'Sectoral Programmes of Development', *Eighth Five Year Plan 1992-97,* Vol. II, New Delhi: Planning Commission.

Government of India (2002): 'Sectoral Policies and Programmes', *Tenth Five Year Plan 2002-07,* Vol. II, New Delhi: Planning Commission.

Government of India (2006): *Provisional Results of Economic Census 2005: All India Report,* New Delhi: Central Statistical Organisation (*http://www.mospi.gov.in*).

Gupta, M.L. and N. Gupta (2006): 'Economic Empowerment of Women through SHGs'. *Kurukshetra,* Vol. 54, No. 4, pp. 23-26.

Haider, S. (2000): 'Migrant Women and Urban Experience in a Squatter Settlements', In: *Urban Space and Human Destinies* (eds.) V. Dupont, E. Tarlo and D. Vidal, New Delhi: Manohar Publishers and Distributors.

Haque, M. (2006): 'Dhubri Hatchery: Ray of Hope for Self-Help Groups', *Kurukshetra,* Vol. 54, No. 11, pp. 43-44.

Harper, M., A. Berkhof and R.V. Ramakrishna (2005): 'SHG-Bank Linkage: A Tool for Reforms in Cooperatives?', *Economic and Political Weekly,* Vol. XL, No. 17, pp. 1720-25.

Hermes, N. and R. Lensink (2007): 'Impact of Microfinance: A Critical Survey', *Economic and Political Weekly,* Vol. XLII, No. 6, pp. 462-65.

Kalpana, K. (2005): 'Shifting Trajectories in Microfinance Discourse', *Economic and Political Weekly,* Vol. XL, No. 51, pp. 5400-09.

Karmakar, A. (2008): 'Indian Microfinance—An Avenue Towards Human Capital Development', *The Management Accountant,* Vol. 48, No. 11, pp. 827-34.

Karmakar, K.G. (1999): *Rural Credit and Self-Help Groups: Microfinance Needs and Concepts in India,* New Delhi: Sage Publications.

Karmakar, K.G. (2009): 'Emerging Trends in Microfinance', *Economic and Political Weekly,* Vol. XLIV, No. 13, pp. 21-24.

Karner, T.X. (2000): Social Capital. In: *Encyclopedia of Sociology* (eds.) E.F. Bargatta and R.J.V. Montgomery, Vol.4, p. 2638.

Khandelwal, A.K. (2007): 'Microfinance Development Strategy for India', *Economic and Political Weekly,* Vol. XLII, No. 13, pp. 1127-35.

Kluckhohn, Cf.C. (1953): 'Universal Categories of Culture', In: *Anthropology Today* (ed.) A.L. Kroeber, Chicago: Chicago University Press, pp. 507-23.

Korten, D.C. (1990): *Getting to the 21st Century: Voluntary Action and the Global Agenda,* West Hartford: Kumarian Press.

Kumar, V. (2007): 'From Our Desk', *Microfinance Focus,* Vol. 2, No. 1, p. 3.

Lakshmanan, S. (2001): 'Working of Self-Help Groups with Particular Reference to Mallipalayam Self-Help Group, Gobichettipalayam Block, Erode District, Tamil Nadu', *Indian Journal of Agricultural Economics,* Vol. 56, No. 3, p. 457.

Lalith, N. and R. Dayanandan (2005): *NABARD and Rural*

Transformation, New Delhi: Dominant Publishers and Distributors.

Lawson, T. and J. Garrod (2003): *Complete A – Z Sociology Handbook* (3rd Ed.), London: Hodder and Stoughton Educational.

Loganathan, P. and R. Asokan (2006): 'Inter Regional Development of Self-Help Groups in India', *Kurukshetra*, Vol. 54, No. 11, pp. 9-12.

Madheswaran, S. and A. Dharmadhikary (2001): 'Empowering Rural Women through Self-Help Groups: Lessons from Maharashtra Rural Credit Project', *Indian Journal of Agricultural Economics*, Vol. 56, No. 3, pp. 427-43.

Mallick, A (2007): 'Social Mobilisation: An Empowering Tool for Community Development', *Kurukshetra*, Vol. 55, No. 10, pp. 22-25.

Manimekalai, M. and G. Rajeswari (2001): 'Nature and Performance of Informal Self-Help Groups—A Case from Tamil Nadu', *Indian Journal of Agricultural Economics*, Vol. 56, No. 3, p. 453-54.

Marascuilo, L.A. and R.C. Serlin (1988): *Statistical Methods for the Social and Behavioural Sciences*, New York: W.H. Freeman and Company.

Maxim, P.S. (1999): *Quantitative Research Methods in the Social Sciences*, Oxford: Oxford University Press.

Mehra, A.K. (1991): *The Politics of Urban Redevelopment: A Study of Old Delhi*, New Delhi: Sage Publications.

Mehrotra, S. and S. Mathur (2006): 'Growth of Institutional Credit', *Kurukshetra*, Vol. 54, No. 11, pp. 21-24.

Mishra, A. (2006): 'Microfinance in India and Millennium Development Goals: Maximising Impact on Poverty', *Discussion Paper for the Workshop on World Bank, Singapore*, (September 18).

Moser, C.A. (1969): *Survey Methods in Social Investigation*, Heinemann Educational Books Ltd.

Mukherjee, D. (2007): 'Relevance of Micro Credit: Bangladesh

Example Needs to be Emulated', *Kurukshetra*, Vol. 55, No. 3, pp. 31-32.

Mustafa, K.; Z.A. Gill and T. Azid (2000): 'NGOs, Microfinance and Poverty Alleviation: Experience of the Rural Poor in Pakistan', *The Pakistan Development Review*, Vol. 39, No. 4, Part II, pp. 771-92 *(http://www.pide.org.pk/pdf)*.

Nair, T.S. (2005): 'The Transforming World of Indian Microfinance', *Economic and Political Weekly*, Vol. XL, No. 17, pp. 1695-98.

Namboodiri, N.V. and R.L. Shiyani (2001): 'Potential Role of Self-Help Groups in Rural Financial Deepening', *Indian Journal of Agricultural Economics*, Vol. 56, No. 3, pp. 401-9.

National Bank for Agriculture and Rural Development (NABARD) (1999): '*Gender Equality: Empowerment of Rural Women through NABARD Schemes*', Mumbai: NABARD.

National Bank for Agriculture and Rural Development (NABARD) (2008): *Report on the Committee of Financial Inclusion*, Mumbai: NABARD *(www.nabard.org/pdf/report_financial/Full%20Report.pdf)*.

Padmavathi, D. (2008): 'Empowerment of Women through Microfinance', In: *Empowerment in India: Vision for 21st Century* (ed.) R. Pandya, New Delhi: New Century Publications, pp. 331-40.

Pandey, D.D. (2007): 'Social Capital and Development', *Kurukshetra*, Vol. 55, No. 10, pp. 26-29.

Pandey, V. (2007): 'Urban Microfinance—Efforts towards a Lasting Impact', *Microfinance Focus*, Vol. 2, No. 1, pp. 4-9 *(http://www.karmayog.org/redirect/strred.asp?docId=10337)*.

Pant Joshi, D. (2010): *Microfinance for Macro Change Emerging Challenges*, New Delhi: Gyan Publishing House.

Pearce, D.W. and J.J. Warford (1993): *World without End: Economics, Environment and Sustainable Development*, New York: Oxford University Press.

Pearce, J. (2005): 'Development, NGOs and Civil Society: The Debate and its Future', In: *Development, NGOs and Civil Society*, Jaipur: Rawat Publications, pp. 15-43.

Peck, L. (2005): *Delhi: A Thousand Years of Building,* New Delhi: The Lotus Collection.

Pillai, B.V. and V. Harikumar (2006): 'Self-Help Groups in Kerala', *Kurukshetra,* Vol. 54, No. 9, pp. 30-32.

Prasad, B.D. and S. Haranath (2004): 'Micro Credit through Self-Help Groups: A Strategy in Poverty Alleviation', In: *Census 2001 and Human Development in India* (eds.) G. Ramachandrudu and M.P. Rao, New Delhi: Serials Publications, pp. 460-69.

Priya, R. (2006): 'Town Planning, Public Health and Delhi's Urban Poor: A Historical Review', In: *Urban Studies* (eds.) S. Patel and K. Dev, New Delhi: Oxford University Press, pp. 223-245.

Puhazhendhi, V. and K.J.S. Satyasai (2001): 'Economic and Social Empowerment of Rural Poor through Self-Help Groups', *Indian Journal of Agricultural Economics,* Vol. 56, No. 3, pp. 450-51.

Radhakrishna, R. and S. Ray (2005): 'Poverty in India: Dimensions and Character', In: *India Development Report 2004-05* (ed.) K.S. Parikh and R. Radhakrishna, Oxford University Press and Indira Gandhi Institute of Development Research, pp. 40-61.

Ragin, C.C. (1994): *'Constructing Social Research: The Unity and Diversity of Method',* California: Pine Forge Press *(http://en.wikipedia.org/wiki/Social_research).*

Rajasekhar, D. and R.R. Biradar (2004): *Reluctant Partners Coming Together? Interface between People, Government and the NGOs,* New Delhi: Concept Publishing Company.

Rajasekhar, D., N.K. Gowda and R. Manjula (2006): *Impact of Bank Interest Rates on SHG Members,* New Delhi: Concept Publishing Company.

Rajkumar, K.P. (2006): 'Dedicated Service of NABARD to the Nation', *Kurukshetra,* Vol. 54, No. 11, pp. 17-20.

Ramesh, T. (2008): 'Microfinance—A Drive to Combat Poverty', *The Management Accountant,* Vol. 48, No. 11, pp. 822-26.

Rath, N. (2007): 'On the Microfinance Regulation Bill 2007', *Economic and Political Weekly*, Vol. XLII, No. 37, pp. 3692-97.

Rath, N. (2008): 'Microfinance Regulation Bill: A Rejoinder', *Economic and Political Weekly*, Vol. XLIII, No. 19, pp. 84-85.

Reserve Bank of India (2008): *Annual Report 2007-08*, Mumbai: RBI.

Roy Choudhury, S. (2003): 'Old Classes and New Spaces: Urban Poverty, Unorganised Labour and New Unions', *Economic and Political Weekly*, Vol. XXXVIII, No. 50, pp. 5277-84.

Sahoo, R.K. (2008): 'Microfinance and Empowerment of the Poor', In: *Microfinance and Rural Development in India* (eds.) S.K. Das, B.P. Nanda and J. Rath, New Delhi: New Century Publications.

Salamon, L.M. and H.K. Anheier (1994): *Emerging Sector: The Non-profit Sector in Comparative Perspective—An Overview*, Baltimore: John Hopkins University, Institute for Policy Studies.

Sankaran, P.N. (2006): 'Rural Labour Banks: Promoting Employment Generation', *Kurukshetra*, Vol. 54, No. 11, pp. 29-33.

Sarangi, N. (2007): *'Microfinance and the Rural Poor: A Study of Group-based Credit Programmes in Madhya Pradesh, India'*, Ph.D. Thesis, New Delhi: Jawaharlal Nehru University.

Sarantakos, S. (1994): *Social Research*, London: The Macmillan Press Ltd.

Sarkar, D. (2008): 'Indian Microfinance: Lessons from Bangladesh', *Economic and Political Weekly*, Vol. XLIII, No. 1, pp. 18-20.

Satish, P. (2001): 'Some Issues in the Formation of Self-Help Groups', *Indian Journal of Agricultural Economics*, Vol. 56, No. 3, pp. 410-18.

Satish, P. (2005): 'Mainstreaming of Indian Microfinance', *Economic and Political Weekly*, Vol. XL, No. 17, pp. 1731-39.

Schreiner, M. and H.H. Colombet (2001): 'From Urban to

Rural: Lessons for Microfinance from Argentina', *Development Policy Review*, Vol. 19, No. 3, pp. 339-54.

Sen, S. (1999): 'Some Aspects of State NGO Relationships in India in the Post-Independence Era', *Development and Change*, Vol. 30, No. 2, pp. 327-55.

Sharma, R.M. (1988): *Research Methods in Social Sciences*, New Delhi: National Book Organisation.

Shashi, S.S. (ed., 1992) *Encyclopaedia of Humanities and Social Sciences*, New Delhi: Anmol Publications.

Shigetomi, S. (2002): 'The State and NGOs: Issues and Analytical Framework', In: *The State and NGOs: Perspective from Asia* (ed.) S. Shigetomi, Singapore: Institute of Southeast Asian Studies, pp. 1-33.

Shukla, D. (2008): 'Issues of Poverty and Empowerment of Women through SHGs (Self-Help Groups) and Bank-Linkage Programme (NABARD)', In: *Women Empowerment: The Substantial Challenges* (ed.) J.K. Soni, Delhi: Authorspress, pp. 59-70.

Sills, D.L. (1968): 'Voluntary Association: Sociological Aspects', *International Encyclopaedia of Social Sciences*, New York: The Macmillan Company and The Free Press, Vol. 16, pp. 362-79.

Singh, Y. (1973): *Modernization of Indian Tradition (A Systemic Study of Social Change)*, Delhi: Thomson Press (India) Limited.

Singh, Y. (1986): *Modernisation of Indian Traditions: A Systemic Study of Social Change*, Jaipur: Rawat Publications.

Sinha, F. (2005): 'Access, Use and Contribution of Microfinance in India: Findings from a National Study', *Economic and Political Weekly*, Vol. XL, No. 17, pp. 1714-19.

Siwach, R.K. (2004): *Voluntary Organisations and Social Welfare*, Delhi: Shankar Publications.

Slesnick, D.T. (1993): 'Gaining Ground: Poverty in the Post-war United States', *Journal of Political Economy*, Vol. 101, pp. 1-38.

Soni, A. (2006): 'Urban Conquest of Outer Delhi Beneficiaries, Intermediaries and Victims: The Case of Mehrauli Countryside', In: *Urban Studies* (eds.) S. Patel and K. Dev, New Delhi: Oxford University Press, pp. 294-317.

Soundarapandian, M. (2006): 'Micro Finance for Rural Entrepreneurs: Issues and Strategies', *Kurukshetra*, Vol. 54, No. 11, pp. 14-16.

Srinivas, M.N. (1955): 'The Social System of a Mysore Village', In: *Village India.* (ed.) Mckim Marriott, Chicago: University of Chicago Press.

Srinivas, M.N. (1962): 'A Note on Sanskritization and Westernization', In: *Caste in Modern India and other Essays*, London: Asia Publishing House.

Srinivas, M.N. (1987): *The Dominant Caste and other Essays*, Delhi: Oxford University Press.

Sriram, M.S. (2005): 'Microfinance and the State: Exploring Areas and Structures of Collaboration', *Economic and Political Weekly*, Vol. XL, No. 17, pp. 1699-1704.

Sriram, M.S. and R. Kumar (2007): 'Conditions in which Microfinance has Emerged in Certain Regions', *Economic and Political Weekly*, Vol. XLII, No. 49, pp. 67-72.

SU (2007): 'From Marginal Tinkering to Major Changes: Microfinance and Poverty Alleviation', *Economic and Political Weekly*, Vol. XLII, No. 5, pp. 349-52.

Supriti, S.M. Barnhardt and R. Ramanathan (2002): *'Urban Poverty Alleviation in India: A General Assessment and a Particular Perspective'*, Vol.1, Bangalore: Ramanathan Foundation (*http://unpan1.un.org/intradoc/groups/public/documents/APCITY/UNDPANO029047.pdf*).

Tarafdar, P. (2008): 'Policies and Programmes for Women's Empowerment in the South Asian Context', In: *New Dimensions of Women Empowerment* (ed.) A.K. Sinha, New Delhi: Deep and Deep Publications Pvt. Ltd., pp. 25-39.

***The Economic Times*,** 8th August., 2008 (*http://www.ncaer.org/downloads/MediaClips/Press/Ecotimes-top20citieshold. pdf*).

The Times of India, 22nd July, 2006 (*http://timesofindia.indiatimes.com/articleshow/1789927.cms*).

Tilekar, S.N.; N.J. Naikade; B.J. Deshmukh and A.A. Patil (2001): 'Women Self-Help Groups Affiliated to 'Chaitanya': A Study on Pune District', *Indian Journal of Agricultural Economics*, Vol. 56, No. 3, p. 458.

Tripathy, K.K. (2006): 'Micro-credit Intervention and Poverty Alleviation', *Kurukshetra*, Vol. 54, No. 11, pp. 4-8.

United Nations Environment Programme (2003): '*Microfinance in the Urban Environmental Development Perspective*', International Environmental Technology Centre (*www.unep.or.jp/ietc/focus/Microfinance-interlinkages.doc*).

Vasimalai, M.P. and K. Narender (2007): 'Microfinance for Poverty Reduction: The Kalanjiam Way', *Economic and Political Weekly*, Vol. XLII, No. 13, pp. 1190-95.

Vatta, K. and P. Singh (2001): 'The Performance of Self-Help Groups in Punjab: A Study of Hoshiarpur District', *Indian Journal of Agricultural Economics*, Vol. 56, No. 3, p. 452.

Vatta, K. (2003): 'Microfinance and Poverty Alleviation', *Economic and Political Weekly*, Vol. XXXVIII, No. 5, pp. 432-33.

Verma, R. (2008): 'Microfinance and Empowerment of Rural Women', *Kurukshetra*, Vol. 56, No. 11, pp. 3-5.

Verma, U. (2001): *Delhi: A Tale of Seven Cities*, New Delhi: Smriti Books.

Verman, P.M. (2005): 'Impact of Self-Help Groups on Formal Banking Habits', *Economic and Political Weekly*, Vol. XL, No. 17, pp. 1705-13.

Vijaykumar, R. (2009): 'Reinstating the Self-Help Group Perspective in Microfinance', *Economic and Political Weekly*, Vol. XLIV, No. 15, pp. 68-69.

Wiser, W.H. (1936/1969): *The Hindu Jajmani System: A Socio-Economic System Interrelating Members of a Hindu Village Community*, Lucknow: Lucknow Publishing House.

Wolch, J.R. (1990): *The Shadow State: Government and the Voluntary Sector in Transition*, New York: The Foundation Centre.

World Bank (1999): *Bangladesh: From Counting the Poor to Making the Poor Count*, Washington, D.C.: The World Bank.

World Bank (2005): *World Development Report*, Washington D.C.: Oxford University Press.

Yadagiri, M. and V. Gangadhar (2008): 'Microfinance: The Emerging Horizons', *The Management Accountant*, Vol. 48, No. 11, pp. 816-21.

Yadav, S.S. (2006): 'Self-Help Group Movement in Rajasthan: Bright Prospects', *Kurukshetra*, Vol. 54, No. 11, pp. 26-28.

Yunus, M. (2004): 'Grameen Bank, Microcredit and Millennium Development Goals', *Economic and Political Weekly*, Vol. XXXIX, No. 36, pp. 4077-80.

Yunus, M. (2007): *Banker to the Poor*, New Delhi: Penguin Books.

Websites

http://en.wikipedia.org

http://proquest.umi.com

http://ssrn.com

http://timesofindia.indiatimes.com

http://unpan1.un.org

http://www.chillibreeze.com

http://www.developmentgateway.com.au

http://www.engagingcommunities2005.org

http://www.grameen-info.org

http://www.indiatogether.org

http://www.info.gov.za

http://www.jstor.org

http://www.krpcds.org

http://www.microfinancegateway.org

http://www.msdf.org

http://www.mumbaispace.com

http://www.ncaer.org

http://www.ndmc.gov.in

http://www.pide.org.pk

http://www.planning.kar.nic.in

http://www.rbi.org.in

http://www.socialresearchmethods.net

http://www.usaid.gov

http://www.webref.org

www.epidemiolog.net

www.grameenfoundation.org

www.nabard.org

www.solutionexchange-un.net.in

www.uncdf.org

www.unep.or.jp

Index